Preaching The Funeral Homily

Proclaiming the Gospel Of Heavenly Hope

R. C. Sonefeld

Foreword by Andrew Greeley

Resource Publications, Inc.
San Jose, California

Reprint Department
Resource Publications, Inc.
160 E. Virginia Street #290
San Jose, CA 95112-5876
(408) 286-8505 (voice)
(408) 287-8748 (fax)

Library of Congress Cataloging-in-Publication Data

Sonefeld, R. C. (Raymond Christopher), 1921–
  Preaching the funeral homily : proclaiming the gospel of heavenly hope /
  R. C. Sonefeld; foreword by Andrew Greeley.
    p. cm.
  Includes bibliographic references.
  ISBN 0-89390-480-5 (pbk.)
  1. Funeral sermons. 2. Sermons, American. I. Title.
BV4275 .S553 2000
252'. 21; aa05 12-17—dc99   99-088468

Printed in the United States of America.
  01 02 03 04 | 5 4 3 2

Editorial director: Nick Wagner
Project coordinator: Mike Sagara
Copyeditor: Robin Witkin

To My Sister, Sue

For this we say unto you by the word of the Lord, that we which are alive and remain unto the coming of the Lord shall not prevent them which are asleep.

For the Lord himself shall descend from heaven with a shout, with the voice of the archangel, and with the trump of God: and the dead in Christ shall rise first:

Then we which are alive and remain shall be caught up together with them in the clouds, to meet the Lord in the air: and so shall we ever be with the Lord.

Wherefore comfort one another with these words.

1 Thessalonians 4:15 (KJV)

Contents

The Composition of the Funeral Homily
The Do's of Homily Preaching
The Don'ts of Homily Preaching
Use of Poetry

   Acceptance of Death
   Consolation
   Death
   Fear of Death
   Denial of God
   Devil
   Disbelief
   Funeral Eulogies
   Grief
   Heaven
   Holy Humor
   Humorous Stories
   Immortality
   Philosophy of Life
   Preaching
   Purpose of Life
   Resurrection
   Soul

   Builders of Eternity
   I Did Not Die
   The Devil Is a Gentleman
   Death of a Child

Acknowledgments

I would like to thank Monsignor Francis J. Murray, MA, of the Saginaw Diocese, and Edward Majzlik, MS, of Aiken, South Carolina, for the preparation and editing of these homilies.

Grateful acknowledgment is extended to the following copyright holders for granting permission to reprint copyrighted material:

Excerpt from W. H. AUDEN: COLLECTED POEMS by W. H. Auden, edited by Edward Mendelson. Copyright © 1940 and renewed 1968 by W. H. Auden. Reprinted by permission of Random House, Inc.

Excerpts from the English translation of *Order of Christian Funerals* © 1985, International Committee on English in the Liturgy, Inc. All rights reserved.

Excerpts from "When a Loved One Dies" by Betsy Kennedy reprinted with permission from *The Voice* ([31 May 1995]: 12).

Selections by Rev. John B. Healey (26 November 1988) and by William A Berry, SJ (28 November 1987) are reprinted with permission from *America*.

Selection from *Timely Homilies: The Wit and Wisdom of an Ordinary Pastor* (paper, 176 pp., $9.95), copyright 1990 by William J. Bausch, published by Twenty-Third Publications, P.O. Box 180, Mystic, CT 06355, is reprinted with permission. Toll free: 1-800-321-0411.

Malcolm Muggeridge quotation from *National Review* (December 31, 1990), 24. © 1990 by National Review, Inc., 215 Lexington Avenue, New York, NY 10016. Reprinted by permission.

Biblical quotations or paraphrases are taken from or based on the New Revised Standard Version of the Bible, copyrighted, 1989 by the Division of Christian Education of the National Council of the Churches of Christ in the United States of America, and are used by permission. All rights reserved.

Acknowledgments

Many of the quotations herein are taken from *Bartlett's Familiar Quotations*, 16th ed. (Boston: Little, Brown and Co., 1992); *Christopher News Notes*, various issues (New York: The Christophers); *20,000 Quips and Quotes* (New York, 1968); *Book of Catholic Quotations* (Cudahy, New York: Farrar, Strauss, 1956); *Peter's Quotations: Ideas for Our Times* (New York: Morrow, 1993).

In the event that some source or copyright holder has been overlooked, please send acknowledgment requirements to the editorial director at Resource Publications, Inc.

Foreword

There is a dangerous asymmetry in the relationship between the minister and the mourners at a funeral liturgy. For the mourners the liturgy is usually a moment of grief and pain, a unique and critically important experience in their lives. For the minister the funeral liturgy can easily become just one more funeral that disrupts his morning and jumbles an already too busy daily schedule.

Moreover the minister might well feel that there is just so much grief one can absorb in one's life. To try to pretend to the mourner's same grief several times a month and often several times a week is beyond human capability. The mourners expect healing and reassurance, but personalized healing and reassurance. The minister, rushing through the demands of the day, is inclined to fall back on a homily that has often been delivered before, one which is sincere but has perhaps become shopworn from frequent repetition and which some of the parishioners may have heard before, maybe many times before.

I describe this asymmetry with no intent to criticize the minister involved. But there is so little time in a day and so little opportunity to rethink the issue of the funeral homily.

Father Sonefeld has therefore done a very good work for all of us in preparing this volume of homiletic paradigms for the Eucharist of the Resurrection. At a minimum his homilies will challenge us to rethink our routine responses to the funeral liturgy. More than that, the homilies in this book of paradigms will provide many priests with insights and ideas for constructing their own repertory of homilies for these occasions, homilies which can be revised and reconstructed almost at the last minute to make the communication from pulpit to congregation alive, meaningful, and healing.

I suspect that many mourners in years to come will profit from this book, though they may not know of its existence.

Andrew Greeley
Chicago
Feast of the Little Flower

Introduction

Probably there is no training that can adequately prepare someone for the important task of preaching the funeral homily. Some have a talent and a feeling for preaching in any situation. They exhibit ease and poise whenever they preach at a funeral. They know what to say and what to avoid. Others must acquire these skills by firsthand experience. Also, study and work can achieve a high degree of proficiency. Plenty of resources are available.

Preparation is always necessary. Somebody must sweat, either the preacher in the preparation, or the assembly during the delivery. Think of the assembly—that is the first rule.

Writing a funeral homily is hard work, but it is rewarding. Dealing with death is the most stressful event in life. This naturally painful experience is endured by all humanity; the loss of a loved one or a friend, and the ensuing process of picking up the pieces and returning to daily routine, deserves help from the Gospel. The aftereffects of grief, depression, loneliness, and despair—all calling for the new adjustment—shape the purpose of the homily.

The homily is a noble, worthy project in assisting people with the distressing anxieties of death and dying. Overwhelming sympathy and exemplary patience are expected from the preacher. In a sense, the preacher is putting Christianity on trial, and thus through the very best anyone can muster, this should be a primary concern. Compassion and empathy must be evident. The opportunity for evangelization often calls on the preacher's zeal to help the living and hearten the survivors. A funeral may be the only occasion when a given person enters the boundaries of a church. For many people, too, the death of a cherished person presents the most compelling recognition one can have of one's own death to come. John Donne reflects the same insight in his famous sermon, "And therefore never send to know for whom the bell tolls; it tolls for thee." There will be occasions when even the experienced homilist will be so moved by grief, affection, or the obvious emotions of the worshipers that he may depart from some of his prepared material. Memories and phrases from years of preaching will well up in his mind, and he will rise to the occasion. When the homily is worked over in the office or study, conditions are calm and sedate, but during the actual delivery, inspiration and the Holy Spirit can ignite the homilist. Toward the preparation of the homily, the rules and regulations are listed in the official liturgical source, *Order of Christian Funerals*. The following instruction tells us nothing new in repeating "there is never to be a eulogy":

> A brief homily based on the readings is always given after the Gospel reading at the funeral liturgy and may also be given after the readings at the vigil service; but there is never to be a eulogy. Attentive to the grief of those present, the homilist should dwell on God's compassionate love and on the paschal mystery of the Lord, as proclaimed in the Scripture readings. The homilist should also help the members of the assembly to understand that the mystery of God's love and the mystery of Jesus' victorious death and resurrection were present in the life and death of the deceased and that these mysteries are active in their own lives as well. Through the homily members of the family and community should receive consolation and strength to face the death of one of their members with a hope nourished by the saving word of God. Laypersons who preside at the funeral rites give an instruction on the readings (27).

There is a strong tradition in the church against eulogies. Nothing should be done, the theory goes, to make a difference between people at the time of death. We are all equal in the sight of God, and so there should be the same service, the same words, the same liturgy for everyone. It's tempting to make an exception, and many homilists, carried away by compassion and love, easily rationalize that this person is special. But that would not only break a strong tradition, it would go against the whole purpose of this community of faith believers. What we have been learning these last few years is that people are people. No one person is more precious than another or less precious than another. What we should be doing is thinking about the love and mercy of God, about the way God loves us and the way God asks us to respond. This regulation is well expressed by Father Aidan Ryan in an article that he wrote for the May 1992 issue of *The Furrow*, entitled "The Funeral Liturgy":

> The homily is perhaps the most difficult area of the funeral liturgy in which to strike the right note. The Order, like its predecessors, specifically rules out a eulogy. And yet, one must be in some way personal regarding the deceased. It might be helpful if we understood the funeral liturgy as containing in it an element of thanksgiving to God for His presence in and through the life of the deceased. We thank God for having given the gift of life and for sustaining it for so many years/months/days. We can thank God too for whatever gifts of nature of personality the deceased may have possessed and for whatever good she/he may have done during life. But the emphasis is not on praising the dead, but on thanking the living God (284).

The second instruction of great value is the selected Scripture readings from the Old and New Testaments. Expert Scripture scholars compiled these readings: the first and second readings, the responsorial psalms, the Alleluia verses before the Gospel, and the Gospel readings. The main bulk of the homily should be based on these chosen readings. Other biblical references are secondary and other sources, in a discreet limited way, may be used.

There are several reasons that demand discipline in the funeral homily, without our getting into a debate on the dilemma of eulogy or homily.

The homilist does not have to introduce the deceased to the assembly by a lengthy list of achievements and honors earned in life. The Rev. William J. Bausch makes this observation in his book, *Timely Homilies*:

> Sometimes at funerals we don't talk much about or praise the person who had died, and that is because the funerals, in a sense, are for our benefit—for the living—because you and I have to undergo this experience, and someone's death prepares us for it. And whether we

3

are a Catholic, Protestant, Jew, or atheist, none of us can fail to be moved at this (160).

The structural readings serve the purpose of the church's liturgical empathy to honor rich and poor alike, for in death we are all equal.

To select the three readings without making any references to them dilutes their effectiveness. Christ speaks to us and is present through his revealed word. How often does it happen that if you asked one or more members of the assembly what the readings were, they have no recollection. There is a big advantage in this reinforced repetition. The familiar consoles, gives stability and conviction to bereaved souls. The homily has the same advantage of reinforcing our hope and conviction of immortality. The current ritual does provide for the more personal reflection on the life of the deceased by a friend or family member at the end of the Eucharist, before the final blessing or commendation.

Besides the mandated rules, I would make some practical suggestions from my own experience and from my research reading:

Step 1. Contact the family. The pre-funeral visit is more than an act of kindness. This can often be done when the family comes in to make the funeral arrangements. If the mortician makes this approach, then the homilist must contact the family. This contact will generate untold gratitude and appreciation from the bereaved. Even a short follow-up visit frequently will enhance your act of charity in their memories.

Contact is necessary for emotional analyses of the bereaved's state of coping with their grief. During this visit, observe their emotional state, the low and high thresholds. Also, look for such signs as anger, fear, anxiety, shock, equanimity of faith, gratitude for a happy death, surprise at a premature death, or withdrawal from outside intervention. Usually these feelings are not subtle or hidden. They are spontaneous reactions, especially when religious intervention is offered.

Step 2. From the emotional evaluation comes the specificity of the Scripture application to the deceased and his or her loved ones. In newspaper writing, the specifics are usually referred to as what, where, why, when, and how—the backbone of all writing and speaking. This personal information leads to the selection of the scriptural texts.

Respect and consideration should be given to each deceased and to each group of mourners. Even though the same texts are used, the language and additional subject matter are adapted to *this* individual and *this* family, unique and different.

Despite the commonalities of the human grief experience, more is expected besides the obvious importance of the name of the deceased. Family names will be mentioned, as well as the relationship of the deceased with the parish, community, and social and civic affiliations (if noteworthy), and the significant contributions of the deceased's life. As is stated in *Funeral Liturgies*:

> Since each person is unique, each liturgy should, to some degree, be special. Hence it is essential to know at least a fragment of the biography of the deceased. In fact, the more we know about the deceased the better. The funeral rites should not concern themselves exclusively with the death of the deceased, but should be a celebration of his/her life (McCarthy 11).

A caution quickly comes to mind. Let's not exaggerate or overdo the grief and anxiety. The liturgy of the Mass of Christian Burial, the readings, and the homily are directed to strengthen and console, reflecting built-in concern for normal assemblies and bereaved loved ones. Support groups and professional assistance are the general routes for survivors who can't cope.

Scientifically, the Holmes Stress Scale rates the obvious. Death is number one. Scripture echoes the same reaction. St. Paul reminds us of this truth in 1 Corinthians 15:56–57, "The sting of death is sin, and the power of sin is the law. But thanks be to God, who gives us the victory through our Lord Jesus Christ." Christians are not supposed to fool themselves into thinking death does not hurt. It does. It always will. But for the Christian, that isn't the whole story. What we have done or failed to do makes for the hurt. What God has done in Jesus Christ gives us the victory nonetheless.

Step 3. Reading: Publishers can supply a wealth of ideas and material. Take time to scrutinize what exists in print.

The dean of the preacher's teachers, Father Walter Burghardt, SJ, certifies the vast scope of homiletic resources (quoted by William Bole, "The Preacher's Teacher," *Our Sunday Visitor* 9 [June 1996]: 12):

> What I try to tell the priests is: Your homily is all around you, from the moment you go to bed. It's the meditations you make. It's the people you meet. It's the hospital you visit, the TV you watch, the books you read.

Step 4. Remote preparation: Prayer and meditation from daily spiritual practices. This is an ongoing life process. Plato recognized that when he wisely wrote, "All philosophy is a meditation on death."

The Composition of the Funeral Homily

To put it bluntly: Homilies should be interesting, appealing, substantive, and challenging. Content is a necessity. Scripture is an indispensable foundation, the sine qua non. But supplement it with your own background of knowledge from other sources, since all truth derives from God. Whatever happens to be your purview: the humanities, science, the treasure of the saints, personal anecdotes. Pope John Paul II, in his 1980 Holy Thursday letter to priests, endorsed nonscriptural excerpts which can be profitable in the homily:

> Indeed, the homily is supremely suitable for the use of such texts provided their content corresponds to the required conditions, since it is one of the tasks that belong to the nature of the homily to show the point of convergence between revealed wisdom and noble human thought seeking truth by various paths.

A good, pertinent quotation, either scriptural or from human sources, will help guarantee a satisfactory homily. Two minds are usually stronger than one. Don't hesitate to lean on these sources.

In quoting either a biblical text or other sources, the homilist must adjust both the pace and the voice level to accommodate the change from the normal, usual speech pattern. The quotation, either read or memorized, must stand by itself, and it must be given in a special voice to call attention to it. Otherwise, it may be wasted. This could result in this syndrome, "What did he say? I missed much of it." The mind distracted in trying to recall the quotation equals a mental disturbance. So pause, raise or lower the voice, and slow down the pace.

The unwritten rule of ten minutes for weekend homilies does not apply to funeral homilies. Funerals are different. The family and friends are all at the Mass of Christian Burial by choice, not out of obligation but out of love and friendship. They are there to share the grief of the family and to give closure to bereavement. They are involved because their emotions are focused on the deceased and on their own future summons. So the homilist has leverage on time limits. One rule might be: Be brief, no matter how long it takes. Your homily may take from ten to seventeen minutes (while you remain aware of the law of diminishing returns). Mourners want to listen to an interesting sermon, to be encouraged. If you are good, ten or even seventeen minutes will be too short. If you observe the assembly, you will sense when you should leave the pulpit for the altar.

The Do's of Homily Preaching

Above all, be yourself. Don't try to be another Bishop Fulton J. Sheen or Rev. Billy Graham. In 1959, e. e. cummings responded to a high school news editor who wanted advice for young people desiring to write poetry. What Cummings advised can be transferred to the preacher. "To be nobody—but yourself—in a world which is doing its best, night and day, to make you everybody else—means to fight the hardest battle which any human being can fight and never stop fighting" (quoted by James H. Laird, "The Pangs and Pitfalls of Pulpitry," *Detroit Free Press* 15 [August 1965]: 21). Being yourself indicates sincerity.

Be simple. You need to be understood by the assembly, even by children. It's a compliment to have a youngster or an adolescent remark, "I liked your homily" or "I understood what you said."

Obscurity of expression is surely no guarantee of wisdom, but often its opposite. Clarity is the first rule of communication. If preaching isn't clear, it is wasted. Gauge yourself, as always, to your listeners and speak accordingly. No talking down, no orating over the heads of the assembly. But as a minister of Christ, you're requested to echo the message of resurrection hope. On the occasion of death, spiritual wisdom must dominate and it must further the cause of Christ. Doubts should not be suggested, but always the certainty of faith. This is the time for infallibility and the truth, "I am the resurrection and the life" (Jn 11:25). Death should not alienate anyone from God.

Speak kindly of the deceased. The universal Latin maxim holds sway, *De Mortuis Nihil Nisi Bonum*. If in life kindness has power and charity, so in death it is essential. Grievers look for and yearn for the warmth of Christ. Confidentiality is the privilege of the deceased and of his or her family. Leave the skeletons undisturbed, long buried in the family closet. Of course, into everyone's life a little rain must fall. How well the deceased managed to weather it may reveal life's triumphs. Whatever made that life precious to loved ones and faithful to Christ should be noteworthy. No two lives are identical. Each person faces the struggles of life in a unique way.

The Don'ts of Homily Preaching

Don't give the impression that you composed your homily as you marched down the aisle to bless the coffin, while you were processing to the altar, or even while you were washing and shaving in the morning.

Exaggerations can prove to be embarrassing. Don't get carried away. Kindness need not be insincere. In any case, realism is more genuine. Mourners and friends will be offended by excessive praise. Never display bad taste. Some families even ask for extra restraint, insuring against such lavish references. So respect the wishes of the family. They may inform you of what they object to. That's why a personal visit with the family is vital. You might ask them about this matter. At times a person will specify in his or her will requests of some do's and don'ts for the funeral. So don't canonize the deceased; leave that process to the church.

> Here two extremes are to be avoided. The first is to speak in abstractions and generalities, without any references to the deceased. The second is to turn the homily into a eulogy of the deceased compounding matters by couching it in exaggerated terms (McCarthy 12).

Do not rush the mourners out too soon. They need to absorb the spiritual uplift and challenge from the homily and the balm from the Eucharist. The Eucharist is a declaration of the deceased's predestination into eternal life, and it correlates your own fate with God. Give the Holy Spirit a chance to invade their minds. So cautions Mother Teresa, "Never let anything so fill you with sorrow as to make you forget the joy of Christ Risen." To paraphrase a common quotation: Let the mourners smell the incense and feel the holy water of their own baptism into the new life of Christ.

Be wary of professionalism or arrogance. Professionalism rises to the surface, whether in the lack of preparation of the homily or in offhandedness in dealing with the feelings and concerns of the bereaved.

Use of Poetry

Poetry can be effective if used properly. But the applicability must be understood by the family and other mourners. Otherwise, its use may result in irritation and criticism. Keep in mind, however, that any need to explain poetry to others dilutes the quality. Poetry is subjective and by nature lends itself to private interpretation. If the homilist is skillful enough in sounding out the deeper meanings, he can share his own understanding, although others may not have perceived it in the same fashion.

Forthright poetry of the classic variety, well known to most people, presents no problem. But some of the modern compositions may do so. Caution should be exercised. By no means should poetry be used for its own sake, to impress others, or to heighten the stature of the homilist. The homilist should never seek his personal enhancement. His purpose is to assuage the grief and sorrow of the mourners. If the poem conveys that purpose, reflecting the mourners' deeper feelings, it can reflect an empathetic understanding. The deceased may have been fond of a poem, may even have composed one; in such cases, the poem might be judged appropriate.

Poetry may turn off some persons, but if it is meaningful to the deceased and family, it is useful despite some general awkwardness.

The following short selections may serve as samples that vividly grapple with the feelings of a death-loss. The majesty of poetry surpasses that of prose. Shakespeare is proof of this power. So are these lines by Edna St. Vincent Millay in her poem "Dirge Without Music."

> I am not resigned to the shutting away of loving hearts
>   in the hard ground.
> So it is, and so it will be, for so it has been time out of mind.
> Into the darkness they go, the wise and the lovely.
> Crowned with lilies and laurels they go; but I am not resigned.
> Lovers and thinkers, into the earth with you.
> Be one with the dull, the indiscriminate dust.
> A fragment of what you felt, of what you knew,
> A formula, a phrase remains—but the best is lost.

This graphic poem may be used to temper the guilt feelings of mourners who have not yet reached the point of resignation to God's will. To some degree, we share the emptiness so common to human nature. Time heals wounds, they say. But while waiting, the modern person will know an honest groping for answers.

The poignant loss of a loved one is agonizingly rehearsed and certainly may elicit tears. Feeling the pain would heighten the joy and acceptance of the best which is yet to come in a peaceful, protective life with the Creator. There is no indifference felt and, like the despair of the holy women in the Easter story, happiness may still abound in the conviction of the risen Lord. The greeting was: "Do not weep. Your beloved lives, though unseen." No one denies this poem by Ruth Menzies expresses the feelings experienced by deep love. It can't fail to jar the thoughtfulness of its hearers.

> There was no long parade,
> no muffled drums
> no horse with swinging boots reversed,
> all that day the birds were mute
> while in the deepening night
> the very tides were stilled
> and, one by one,
> the stars went out.

Death has its dignity, without any need of parades. Memory of the loved one is internal, not needing artificial support. According to his view of the death of the deceased and his empathy with loved survivors, the homilist could reflect how this poem locks in on the grief over death as final. The dramatic addition of ritual and state ceremonies may intensify the loss of death, but there is no denying the personal loss. Presence of a firing squad may accentuate the shocking sorrow and certify finality. When the deceased belongs to the public, his career and profession have won him fame; there is no allowing for a personal private ceremony. The following is the first stanza of a poem by W. H. Auden, called "Stop All Clocks":

> Stop all the clocks, cut off the telephone,
> prevent the dog from barking with a juicy bone,
> silence the pianos and with muffled drum
> bring out the coffin, let the mourners come.

Rather pessimistic, isn't it? Yet it hits you in the vitals. It makes you wonder about the lives before such obvious surrender to death and self-pity can prove a useful foil for the Gospel, which can respond to any raw feelings and despair tossed at it. Truth need have no fear of any expressions of the poetic mind.

There is therapy in expressing this belief about death. It brings out into the open what the human mind thinks about death. A type of implosion of the continuation of life and a reunion of love, not oblivion. Let's not hide the dread-filled and often vacuous views of pagan thought. One must allow the pessimistic side to be persuaded of the brighter, saner side of happiness and victory. The Gospel is not afraid of any earthy, negative diatribes.

The wake service could easily set the tone for the use of poetry, made more effective by quoting the entire poem. Time is more available at a wake, in which people come together to console each other and relate anecdotes about the deceased. The garden variety of nonclassic poetry has more personal appeal. Often one of the grandchildren may compose a poem for his or her grandparent. Such family or amateur compositions express both the deep loss and genuine love for the departed.

One of the strongest moments in the funeral liturgy is the burial. Don't ever regard this moment as trivial or ordinary. The last painful farewell should generate a joyous celebration of faith, a mission totally exceeding any secular or pagan festivity.

Of all the words of wisdom that we could quote regarding the preacher's responsibilities in preaching the Gospel of heavenly hope with unselfconscious empathy, the best statement I have seen was volunteered by L. M. Moore, a professional grave digger in Aiken, South Carolina. In "Grave Digging: A Necessary Business" (*Aiken Standard* [22 May 1991]), Moore was quoted,

> You have to remember that no matter how old the person is, no matter how rich a life he had, he left someone behind who is grieving and hurting. For that individual family, this is the only funeral you have today, even if you really have three or more before the day is over. You can't be in a hurry to get away. You have to be sensitive to the family needs.

Death of a Young Wife And Mother

First Reading	Dn 12:1–3
Responsorial Psalm	Ps 129:1–2,3–4,4–6,7–8
Second Reading	Thes 4:13–18
Gospel Acclamation	Jn 11:25,26
Gospel	Jn 11:17–27

I wish to express my heartfelt condolences to Jack and his children, Michael and Megan; to the parents of Alyce, Ken and Emma; tò her two brothers, Ivan and Alvin; and to all the relatives and friends.

Monday morning, June 4, began as a typical day in the life of Alyce Tabor. She was up early to put breakfast on the table, to supervise the washing and dressing of the children, to prepare herself for work, to check if she had the necessary items for Megan's day care center, and to check if Michael had his books. Perhaps she had a second cup of coffee to start her day. Then, after a kiss and a hug from her husband, she packed everything, including her children into the car. She gave a kiss and a hug to Megan at the day care center and a kiss and a hug to Michael at the school. Finally, with all these tasks completed, she drove off to her job. She had been going through this routine five days a week for many years. She was well organized and confident. A day that started out with dispensing the love and care of a mother. She rarely paid any attention to the stress of such a routine. It was all part of her threefold role of mother, wife, and wage earner.

All of us would have bet that Alyce had some forty-plus years to live and that her dreams and ambitions for her family would be fulfilled. She wanted to see her children through grade school, high school, and college, their marriages, and then the grandchildren. Later, she would spend retirement with her husband, Jack. She was not only a wife, but also a daughter to her loving mother and father. Daughters, even though married, often don't really leave home. They can be counted on to help care for their elderly parents. It is a blessing for parents to be helped in their advanced age.

Alyce was on her way to work when tragedy struck. Every time we enter an expressway or a traffic lane, especially in the early morning rush hours, an accident is possible. Events on the road are often beyond our control, regardless of our defensive driving. We live in a world of speed and steel, where technology can be both good and destructive. Mechanical failure. Human errors. Bad road conditions. Carelessness. There are innocent drivers and innocent victims. How often is the innocent victim killed? As she drove to work, a car ran into her car. Possibly, a defective tire rod, maybe a defect in the steel or construction, caused an oncoming car to veer into her car head-on.

Two children lost a mother; a husband became a widower; the parents suffered the loss of their daughter.

Her husband told his story at the vigil service. He said that he and his wife and children went to church on Sunday. That, despite his loss and pain, he bowed his head and heart to God, his Savior and Redeemer. In baptism, both had pledged their lives to Christ; they had committed their trust to God, just as Christ had done to his heavenly Father when he died on the cross. This is the treasure and strength of a dedicated faith.

Both Alyce and Jack loved God in good times and in bad, in life and in death. As Job expressed his trust, "The Lord has given, the Lord has taken away. Blessed be the name of the Lord."

Free will and the eventualities of life are allowed by God to exert their force and consequences, to follow the laws of cause and effect. Death and suffering are evils, contrary to the original will, against the will of God. But God doesn't ordinarily interfere in these casualties nor with the laws of nature. Even to use the expression, as insurance companies do, "an act of God," is incorrect. Destructive storms and upheavals of nature are not positively willed by God, but play their part according to the laws of nature.

St. John's Gospel records Christ's intervention in the death of his friend Lazarus. Christ proved his power over death when he declared, "Lazarus come forth. Destroy this temple and in three days I will rebuild it." Within a week, he would rise from the dead, as he had predicted.

Martha and Mary, the sisters of Lazarus, while waiting for Jesus to come from Perea, the country beyond the Jordan, experienced four days of sadness and grief. When Jesus finally arrived, Martha showed her distress in a mild rebuke to Christ, "If you had been here, my brother would not have died." She was not embarrassed to show her disappointment. She was miffed. Grief claimed her. At the cemetery, tears were shed. Blame was placed on Christ, for not responding immediately: "Why this delay? I believed you could cure my brother."

Christ could have defended himself by explaining that he and his disciples might be stoned by the Judeans for coming to Bethany. Like Martha, all humans react to the death of loved ones with grief and anger. The degree of grief depends on the relationship; the greater the loss, the greater the grief. The passing of grief can't be accelerated. It's like growing up—it takes time. Even though Martha believed in the resurrection and made her profession of faith, she still experienced concern, which is what grief is. "I love this person." "I need this person." So the emotions seek resolution. Did I do enough? If only Christ had been here! Usually no matter what anyone did (or did not do), death would still take place.

Christ had a higher purpose, unknown to Martha, Mary, and his followers. He wanted them to have unshakable proof of his power over death. He declared, "I am the resurrection and the life." Christ was saying it's okay to die. By death you gain your heavenly Father and an everlasting home. Lazarus was one human who died and came back from the grave, with proof that "Christ is the resurrection and the life."

There's an old story, very effective though seldom quoted today, of a conversation between Charles Maurice Talleyrand, the Prime Minister of France, and the French philosopher M. Lepeaux, who invented a new religion which, in his judgment, was superior to Christianity. M. Lepeaux sought from the Prime Minister a revolutionary way to spread his new dynamic religion. Without hesitation Talleyrand replied, "I shall recommend that you have

15

yourself crucified and on the third day rise from the dead." This is the litmus test applied by the divine founder of Christianity, Christ.

Rose Kennedy endured more than the normal amount of grief and pain with the deaths of her four children. The mother of the former President confessed her faith in her Savior, as reported by Cleveland Amory, in *Parade* magazine:

> I have always believed that God never gives a cross to bear larger than we can carry. And I have always believed that, no matter what, God wants us to be happy. He doesn't want us to be sad. Birds sing after a storm. Why shouldn't we?

May the angels lead the soul of Alyce, a faithful Christian wife and mother, into paradise. May the soul of Alyce Tabor and the souls of all the faithful departed, through the mercy of God, rest in peace. Amen.

Death of a Young Husband And Father

I wish to express my heartfelt condolences to Susan on the death of her dear husband, Donald; to their three children, Elizabeth, Shirley, and Brian; to the maternal grandparents, Frank and Odessa Branca; to the paternal grandparents, Ronald and Mary Ann Carpenter; and to the relatives and friends.

At the joyous occasion of a wedding, the young couple is not thinking of death, nor of who will outlive the other. Although death is mentioned in the marriage ceremony, "in sickness and in health, in good times and in bad times, until death do us part," the couple thinks they will live to a ripe old age. Actual statistics would substantiate such thinking. The couple assumes they will not be the exception to the fact and rarely think of a premature separation by death.

Now enter the uncontrollable facts of life: Accident and disease which terminate life prematurely. This is what befell Donald— terminal cancer of the pancreas. He had been reluctant to consult a doctor when he experienced stomach pains. As would most men of thirty-six, he rationalized that it would go away or that it "wasn't too serious."

Donald's wife awoke one morning and discovered that her husband had died in his sleep. Death came to Donald as the Scripture warned, "like a thief in the night." And so, due to the uncertainties of life, young people die just as people in their ripe old age die.

Bishop Fulton J. Sheen wrote a book entitled *Life Is Worth Living.* Even when "death comes like a thief in the night," unexpected or at

17

an early age, Bishop Sheen insisted that life is worth living. Life is always better than no life. Bishop Sheen stated that to be born is to share the best of gifts: God and eternal life. God and eternal life makes life worth living, whether death occurs in the womb or out of the womb—at six, sixteen, thirty-six, or ninety-six. Life of any length is still a gift of God.

The psalmist verifies the value of living with God, "I shall not die but live, and I shall declare the works of the Lord." The truth that Christ was born into this life is proof enough that life is worth living. Christ enjoyed and participated fully in human life, until he freely surrendered his human life, to win our eternal resurrection. We should treasure and enjoy our lives and the lives of our dear ones, as Christ did his human life, for whatever length is granted us.

The philosopher-columnist Sydney J. Harris, syndicated in hundreds of daily papers, once wrote a column entitled, "Despite Mortality, Life's Worth It." In 1962 he wrote about an encounter with a young friend of his, age thirty, who displayed some remarkable wisdom, since his reasoning reflected scriptural honesty. This young man was discussing the death of a dozen or more victims of a collapsed bridge and said, "If I die tomorrow, I would feel I was ahead of the game. I've enjoyed my life, done a lot of things and met a lot of people, and I'm grateful for the experience." The key word here is "grateful." He was accepting the contingency of death. The day was a bonus to him, a gift. The next day did not belong to him. There was no guarantee, no contract for tomorrow.

In making decisions to love a person, a risk is involved. The decision to love is part faith and part trust. Christ risked his life and heavenly glory on the cross to gain the love of each person who was made over in God's image and likeness. Each person is precious in the sight of the Lord, precious enough for Christ to live and die for.

Donald was not a loser, but a winner. In his thirty-six years, he had the quality of a happy life, with a wife and three children. Yet, as we celebrate Donald's union with God, in the Mass of Christian Burial, his family and friends are undergoing the pain of sorrow and mourning. It is normal to experience this emotion in order to gain some kind of balance. A heavy cross has been placed on the family by the loss of a husband and father.

Some wives and mothers have expressed their grief in this manner, "I felt trapped, abandoned, betrayed." Others have experienced these feelings, "Losing a spouse is the most difficult time of one's life. It is like a complete disintegration of your life." Others have said, "I didn't know what grief was. I thought I was going crazy."

What comfort can we give to Susan during her time of loss? Certainly her faith gives her courage to cope with the death of Donald. Our Lord at the Last Supper speaks to Susan in these words, recorded by St. John, which were read this morning, "Let not your heart be troubled. You believe in God, believe also in Me."

In his prologue to the Gospel, St. John says, "In him was life, and the life was the light of all people. The light shines in the darkness, and the darkness did not overcome it." Again John relates, in chapter 14, verse 19, "Because I live, you also will live."

Is life worth living? Think of Donald, who now lives in peace and happiness with the Lord. Ask yourself this question. The answer will have to be yes!

Death of a Young Person
From Leukemia

First Reading	Wis 4:7–14
Responsorial Psalm	Ps 103:8,10,13–14,15–16,17–18
Second Reading	Rom 8:31–39
Gospel Acclamation	Lk 18:16
Gospel	Mk 10:13–16

My heartfelt sympathy goes out to Connie and Otto Harrison; to Charlene's grandparents, June and Delmar Harrison and Darlene and Floyd Boley; to the relatives; to Charlene's classmates; and to her friends.

Perhaps there is nothing that shocks a community more, than the death of a young person. If it is shocking to the general public, how much more to the parents and friends? All the hopes and dreams of parents come to a grinding halt. There is a feeling of unfairness in the death of a young person. We can accept the death of an older person, but not the death of a young person. There is little to be said in the face of such a tragedy.

Charlene died several weeks after she was diagnosed with leukemia. This rare type of blood cancer, in its swiftness, ended Charlene's life at the age of sixteen. Seeing Charlene in the hospital, fighting for her life, sustained hope for a complete recovery. But this was not to be. Medical science could not stem the onslaught of the disease.

Charlene had her whole life ahead of her. She had plans to attend college, pursue a career in nursing, marry, and raise a family.

Her parents' hopes were high, that Charlene would live a long life. Lingering in the minds of Connie and Otto was an uncertainty of whether God would sanction their prayer and request. They devoted their lives to Charlene. Each day, month, and year were times of joy and happiness for Connie and Otto. Charlene gave their lives purpose. A mother's womb can never forget the child that it brought into the world. The father can never forget that together with his wife, a precious child was conceived.

How can Connie and Otto deal with this grief? They must depend on each other and use the resources given to them to get through this traumatic time. Their faith in God will allow them to draw closer together and find relief in the other person's company. By loving each other, they will continue to love Charlene.

During the course of grieving, parents will experience many different emotions. The strongest emotion being anger. There is anger toward medical science for failing to find a treatment that could save their child. There is anger toward God that may appear to be malice, but rather the anger stems from a wounded heart. The grief stage is only temporary. God understands the long and arduous journey parents must make in order to deal with the death of their child.

What funeral could ever overlook St. Paul's exalted manifesto? Paul was not only a problem-solver for his Roman converts, he also followed his own advice. If the solution worked for him, why not for us? Though faced with daily pressures and anxieties regarding his life and the life of his Roman converts, he rose to heavenly heights, by humbly surrendering to his master, Christ. "If God is for us, who is against us? Who will separate us from the love of Christ? Neither the death of an only daughter, nor any tragedies, nor sorrows, nor pain, can separate us from the love of God in Christ Jesus our Lord."

We don't desert God in times of crisis and sorrow. Instead, we admit our absolute reliance to our Savior.

Mark Twain was probably not thinking of this passage of St. Paul when, on a rare occasion, he took a stand for God.

> When I think of the suffering which I see around me, and how it wrings my heart; and then remember what a drop in the ocean this is, compared with the measureless Atlantics of misery which God has to see every day, my resentment is aroused against those thoughtless people who are glib to glorify God, yet never have a word of pity for him (Master Sermon Series).

Connie and Otto will always have precious memories of Charlene. From time to time, they will relive the sixteen years of her life. Beautiful pictures of Charlene sit on the piano and on the mantel. In a drawer lay Mother's Day and birthday cards that they have collected through the years.

Witnessing such a sight drives one to shout "Why, God?" There may be no satisfactory answer, except for the oldest answer in the world: God knows best. St. Paul tried to answer this question with "Nothing can separate us from the love of God." This poem, too, called "Death of a Child," offers an answer:

> I'll lend you for a little while,
> a child of mine, God said,
> for you to cherish while she lives,
> and mourn for when she's dead.
> It may be six or seven years,
> or only two or three,
> but will you, til I call her Home,
> look after her for me?
> She'll bring her love to gladden you,
> and should her stay be brief,
> you'll have a host of memories
> as solace for your grief.
> I cannot promise she will stay,
> since all from earth return,
> but there are lessons taught below
> I want this child to learn.
> I've looked the wide world over
> in my search for teachers true
> and, from the throng
> that crowd life's lane
> at last I've chosen you.
> Now will you give her all your love,
> nor think your labor vain,
> and turn against me when I come
> to take her back again?

Death of a Motor Vehicle Accident Victim

First Reading	Wis 4:7–14
Responsorial Psalm	Ps 129:1–2,3–4,4–6,7–9
Second Reading	Rom 8:31–39
Gospel Acclamation	Jn 3:16
Gospel	Jn 19:27–28,28–30

I wish to express my sincere condolences to Lynn and Howard Pierce on the death of their daughter, Lisa; to her sister, Sibyl, and her brothers, Arthur and Jeffery; to the grandparents; and to her other relatives and friends. Most of you know the details of the tragic death of Lisa, on Saturday evening. Her death is not only a loss and a shock to the family, but to this community and to our parish as well. Her talent and contribution as a journalist will never be forgotten. She will be sadly missed. We thank all of you for attending her funeral and sharing your grief with the Pierce family. Her fiancé, Vincent Fellows, suffered a brain concussion and multiple internal injuries. At this time, his condition is unpredictable. Please keep him in your prayers.

Lisa is irreplaceable. There is nothing in this world that can compensate for the loss of a loved one. A feeling of void and emptiness exists in the hearts of her family and friends. Howard and Lynn would have given up their lives, if it meant their daughter could live. Lisa was too young to die. At twenty-two years of age, Lisa was just beginning her adult life. As a recent graduate, Lisa landed a job at the local paper. Marriage was six months away. Lisa will never experience the joy of marriage, raising children, and building a home for her family. She will never be able to watch her children grow, get married, and have children of their own.

How will Howard and Lynn be able to cope with their daughter's death? Lynn was looking forward to spending her later years surrounded by the love, support, and comfort of all of her children.

Parents live for their children and share in their joy and sorrow. A heavy cross has been placed on her parents' shoulders. Though Lisa's life on earth was cut short, the twenty-two years of her life were not wasted. For twenty-two years, Lisa lived a happy, fun-filled life. She was able to be triumphant during the difficult times. She dreamed of a long and bright future for herself. Howard and Lynn will never forget the twenty-two years spent with their daughter. Those memories are precious.

Life is worth living! Whether we are given one minute or one hundred years, life is worth living! Howard and Lynn gave life to Lisa because of their unselfish cooperation with God. Through baptism, Lisa became an adopted member of God's family. She has been called to receive her inheritance of happiness. These gifts can never be taken away from her. Christ guaranteed that through his death and resurrection; there is the hope of a family reunion.

As Christians, where else can we find a perspective on the tragedy of a premature death? If we listen carefully to the first reading from the Book of Wisdom, we will gain a satisfactory answer. Let's paraphrase the author's truth: The perfection of God can be obtained in a short life. The ideal life is not necessarily a long life.

I think that we can all accept the insight from the Book of Wisdom. Before the fact, we could argue for as long a life as we can get, with the certainty of gaining our salvation by winning the battle over sin and wickedness. But in reality, we must accept, after the fact, a short life imposed on all of us by the uncontrollable accidents of life. Accidents are the relentless risks of life. Prevention, as much as we strive for it, eludes us. Lisa is safe with God, safe from evil and sin, although it was not her choice. Accidents are rarely free choices, except for certain psychological reasons.

We can also benefit from St. Paul's letter to the Romans. We can benefit from St. Paul's experience of consuming anxieties, persecutions, and threats on his life, by striving for the same unwavering faith and reliance in God. No need to push the panic button from despair or gloom. No need to fret. There is both determination and consolation in his advice. It is from this crucible of anxiety that he bursts out with gallant encouragement. He wrote, "If God is for us, who can be against us? What will separate us from the love of Christ? Will anguish, or distress, or persecution, or famine, or peril, or the sword? No ... For I am convinced that neither death, nor life, nor angels, nor principalities, ... nor any other creature will be able to separate us from the love of God in Christ Jesus Our Lord." Howard and Lynn share a portion of their sorrow with Christ in the tragic death of their daughter.

Eternal rest grant unto Lisa Pierce, O Lord, and let perpetual light shine upon her. Amen.

Death of a Divorced Mother

First Reading	Is 25:6–9
Responsorial Psalm	Ps 23
Second Reading	Rv 21:1–5,6–7
Gospel Acclamation	Rv 14:13
Gospel	Jn 17:24–26

I wish to express my sincere sympathy to the parents, Alice and Gerald Clark, on the death of their daughter, Therese; to her brothers, Kenneth and Clyde; and to her son Clyde in Greece who was informed of his mother's death; to her relatives; and to her friends.

Therese's life could be described with this sentence, "Rabboni, when I am dying, how glad shall I be that the lamp of my life has burned out for thee." Therese's family and friends knew the difficult life she led in her later years. The sunshine came early in life. Her later years were quite sad. She was swamped with domestic problems. Perhaps her nature was too tender and delicate. Therese attended Catholic high school. She moved on to college and studied business administration. Her interest lay in travel agencies.

While traveling in Greece, she met her future husband. After they married, they lived in the United States. Her husband became dissatisfied with living in the United States, so she agreed to move to his country. During her stay in Greece, she made a yearly visit to her parents, and they made several trips to Greece. Her son was born in Greece. Her marriage ended after sixteen years. Custody of her son was granted to her ex-husband.

Therese returned to the United States after the divorce. She resumed a successful travel business, which gave her some satisfaction, but despondency nagged her. Her ex-husband remarried. She rarely heard from or saw her son. Her health began to fail. Diagnosed with liver cancer, she eventually had to return home to be with her parents. Death came to Therese at the age of forty-four.

After speaking with her mother, I visited her in the hospital. She was unable to talk. She couldn't accept nourishment by mouth and seemed immobile in bed. I spoke of God to her. I prayed with her. I read the Scriptures. All she did was look at me. All who visited felt instant sympathy toward her. She heard me pray, "Are there any who are sick among you? Let them send for the priests of the church and let the priests pray over them, anointing them with oil in the name of the Lord; and the prayer of faith will save the sick persons, and the Lord will raise them up; and if they have committed any sins, their sins will be forgiven them." So commanded St. James.

Therese deserved a better break in life. God would give her the hope of his own life. The prophet Isaiah foretold, "Lo, this is our God ... for whom we have waited; let us be glad and rejoice in his salvation."

Certainly there is no human wisdom to solve Therese's heartache. Even Oscar Wilde, no champion of religion, admitted the power of God, "How else but through a broken heart can the Lord enter in?" The second reading from the Book of Revelation can lift up all hearts, broken and unbroken, to cloud nine. After twenty chapters of nightmarish battle between angels and dragons, good and evil, life and death, it appears as one of the most beautiful passages in the Scriptures. As the last book of public revelation, you might expect it to be a blockbuster of heavenly hope, the day of God's triumph. Notice the reference, "the sea was no more." In Semitic folklore, the sea was the embodiment of everything wild and rebellious. It was primordial chaos, recalling the ark of Noah and the destruction of the human race, the home of gigantic sea monsters, the belief of Jewish theology of a flat earth and falling off into the sea of death. The Jewish nation was not a nation of mariners, but rather of land lovers. So the assurance of "new heaven and a new earth ... and the sea was no more" was a way of saying that God's work of creation would finally be realized.

This is the beautiful image of a new Jerusalem, "coming down out of heaven from God, prepared as a bride adorned for her husband." Jerusalem represents the whole community as being saved. They have struggled with Jesus to overcome evil with good. They are pictured as having died and gone to their rest with God, but now return home to a new earth. Therese would now be restored as a beautiful bride, enjoying forever the wedding feast of the Lord, which no one could take away. She is safe and loved by her bridegroom, Christ. As a bridegroom delights in his bride, so shall God delight in her.

The same image is presented in the first reading from Isaiah at a wedding feast. "The LORD of hosts will make for all peoples a feast of rich food …. [He] will wipe away the tears from all faces." St. John takes up the theme of Isaiah 65:17, "For I am about to create new heavens [that is, out of already existing heavens] and a new earth [that is, out of existing earth]." The kingdom of God is not an annihilation. It is a transformation. God is not a destroyer. He is a Creator, who makes things whole again, "Behold I make all things new."

The three readings and Psalm 23 infer that in times of suffering and chaos, God will always triumph. In every circumstance of life, though it may be difficult, God knows best. The Book of Revelation still offers God's own encouragement. God will have the last word, which will always be love.

Since Therese was in the travel agency business, language was part of her job. English seems to be a language that seldom conveys the correct depth of our feelings. We must often rely on foreign words. Such is the case with "good-bye." The Italian word *arrivederci*, meaning "until we meet again," says it much better. The first six letters spell the English word *arrive*. It's not good-bye, but an arriving. The French phrase *Au revoir* and the German phrase *auf Wiedersehen* both connote the same meaning. We do not simply say good-bye to Therese, but rather we assure her and ourselves that "we'll meet again." We will arrive again. In our rich faith, the stronger inference is, "We must meet again."

Today, with prayers and hope, we say to Therese, "*Arrivederci*." May God cheer you up and grant you peace and happiness.

Death of a Twice-Married Husband and Father

First Reading	Is 25:6–10
Responsorial Psalm	Ps 23
Second Reading	1 Cor 2:1–6
Gospel Acclamation	Mt 25:34
Gospel	Mt 25:31–37

I wish to express my heartfelt condolences to Kathleen on the death of her dear husband, Dennis; to his children, Danny, Mary Joy, Peter, Dennis Jr., and Sean; to his brother, Anthony; to his sister, Gertrude; to his grandchildren; to his employees; to the public officials in attendance; and to his friends.

Dennis Donohue died late Sunday evening, after suffering a cardiac failure. His firstborn son, Danny, was present at the hospital, along with his second wife, Kathleen. They were witnesses to his obvious suffering. The doctor had already notified them that if Dennis survived, he would be in a persistent vegetative condition. His family prayed that God would spare Dennis a nonfunctioning state of life. Their prayers were answered. Dennis's family is proud of his life of service. The community lost an outstanding citizen. As an employer, he provided a fair livelihood to over three hundred employees.

Dennis Donohue had been anointed in his final hours. Before his heart attack, he had received communion. Throughout his life, celebrating the Eucharist was the center of his spiritual life. Dennis was close to the Lord. Since his retirement, he participated in Mass every day. A place in heaven was reserved for him. Eileen, his first wife, was awaiting him in heaven. We as survivors are told by nature, when a life must come to an end and return to the Creator of life. Death is a passport to eternal life.

Dennis was born and raised in Chicago. He graduated with a degree in business management from Loyola University in Chicago.

He was interested in theology as more than a hobby. Dennis read extensively and was current on religious issues. He engaged in deep conversations on church topics with bishops and clergy.

Twenty-six years ago, I had officiated over the Requiem Mass of his first wife, Eileen. She died at the early age of fifty-six, from cancer of the pancreas. She lingered for some time. During that time, Dennis was a very loving husband. Dennis and Eileen traveled by plane to their favorite spots in Chicago. They even relived their honeymoon night at the Palmer House. No husband could love a wife more than he did.

Dennis remarried Kathleen who was a widow. They had a blissful marriage. Dennis had the greatest amount of happiness allotted to men in this vale of tears. He had the good fortune of sharing his life with two wonderful women. Following retirement, his two sons, Danny and Dennis Jr., took over their father's furniture manufacturing company.

The readings selected by his family reflected the continuation of his earthly happiness in heaven. Heaven was a subject he discussed with me on many occasions. The words of the wedding vows, "until death do us part," are tempered by both the Old Testament writers and the Gospel writers, who record the joys of heaven as similar to the joys of a wedding. This is as close as we might get to what heaven is like. Thoughts such as "a feast of juicy, rich food and pure choice wines" may prove scandalous to some ascetics, but Christ himself used that image, "The kingdom of heaven may be compared to a king who gave a wedding banquet for his son" (Mt 22:2). Psalm 23, the Good Shepherd Psalm, reinforces that belief, "You prepare a table before me … and I shall dwell in the house of the LORD my whole life long."

St. Paul takes us, as usual, to a more lofty, mystical, yet realistic view of heaven. "What no eye has seen, nor ear heard, nor the human heart conceived, what God has prepared for those who love him" (1 Cor 2:9). Be prepared for the biggest surprise of your life! That's why God did not reveal more details. Human nature has no resources for such knowledge.

T. S. Eliot, the English poet laureate and convert to the Catholic faith, contributed his own insight, "Humankind cannot bear very much reality." This is why Christ satisfied the human heart with the image of the banquet. He wanted to suggest a face-to-face vision with God. Faith is your ticket to heaven. Faith is the evidence of things to come and of things unseen. Faith comes through our belief in the word of our munificent Savior.

Dennis Donohue believed and served his master. He now awaits God's confirmation, "Come, you that are blessed by my Father, inherit the kingdom prepared for you from the foundation of the world."

Though Dennis died from heart failure, we can apply what Bob Hope, the "doctor of cheer," recommended as a cure for heart trouble, "The most serious heart trouble is with a person who has no heart to serve the needs of others." Dennis Donohue served God, his family, his church, and his community.

Death of an Unmarried Woman

First Reading	Lam 3:17–26
Responsorial Psalm	Ps 27:1,4,10,13,14
Second Reading	2 Cor 5:1,6–10
Gospel Acclamation	Rv 14:13
Gospel	Jn 6:51–58

I wish to express my heartfelt sympathy to the family of Virginia Nowak; to her sisters, Florence, Dorothy, and Genevieve; to her brothers, Stanley, Ray, and Joseph; to her nieces and nephews; and to her friends.

Virginia was looking forward to being released from the nursing home and returning to her apartment. A nurse informed her that she was steadily improving. After a short stay at the nursing home, Virginia went to the Lord peacefully, in the second week of the new year at the age of eighty-six. Virginia celebrated her last birthday on earth on a Tuesday and died Friday morning.

Virginia was the first child. Through baptism, Virginia and the Lord entered a partnership that would make her an adopted daughter of God, with all the rights to God's kingdom. As she reached the age of judgment, she affirmed the promises made by her parents and godparents. Her life of eighty-six years verified her faithfulness to Christ.

Virginia had a unique life. She was destined to be both mother and father to her three sisters and three brothers. Her mother died after the birth of her third son, Joseph. Within a year, her father, fourteen years older than his late wife, also died. Virginia was now the sole guardian of six children. She was their caretaker, gatekeeper, sole support, and problem solver. Marriage was out of the question. She was too busy to date or even think of deserting her responsibilities. Destiny now dictated her life, which she willingly accepted. If ever there was a cross to bear and at times there must have been, she carried it well. Her joy and happiness would emanate from sacrifice.

There is a very strong tradition in the Church against eulogies. Nothing should be done, the theory goes, to sharpen the differences between people at the time of death. We are all equal in the sight of God. There should be the same service, the same words, the same liturgy for everyone.

It is tempting to make an exception for Virginia by saying that she was special, but that would not only break a strong tradition, it would go against the whole purpose of this parish community. What we've been learning these last few years is that people are people. No one person is more special or less special, more precious or less precious than another. Virginia would certainly, in her humility and modesty, agree with the Church. Whatever the Church recommends would be her wish.

Those closest to Virginia knew that her faith was top priority. This was apparent when she practiced her faith. From the faith given to her at baptism, she believed in the mystery of faith revealed by Christ in the Bible. The words of St. John left no room for doubt, "This is the bread that came down from heaven, not like that which your ancestors ate, and they died. But the one who eats this bread will live forever." Every Sunday at Mass she heard the words of Christ, "This is my body; this is my blood." At the time of death, look into the Bible and you are sure to find comfort in Christ's words. "Those who eat my flesh and drink my blood have eternal life, and I will raise them up on the last day." These words contain the promise and pledge of eternal life. What a comforting message for all of us to hear at the Mass of a departed Christian.

Throughout life, from early youth to the age of eighty-six, Virginia had nourished her soul through celebrating the Eucharist. Virginia was deprived of the support and love of a husband and the joy of bringing her own children into the world. What consoled her? What drove the loneliness out of her life? What provided her with joy in her golden years? There is only one answer. Through her celebration of the Eucharist, she was able to fulfill her obligation as a mother figure to her siblings.

The *Order of Christian Burial* has three Gospel references to the Eucharist as Christ's promise of eternal life. We believe in the words of Christ, "I am the resurrection and the life," and "I am the way, the truth and the life." Furthermore, we infallibly believe in the two clear equations Christ enunciated at the Last Supper when he established a new covenant, "This is my body; this is my blood."

Out of all the gifts Christ could have given us on his last night on earth, he chose the perfect gift. Christ was our gift. The bread and wine that we share during communion, is the Body and Blood of our Lord Jesus Christ. These are visible means of spiritual nourishment for our soul's journey to heaven.

Virginia prayed for a peaceful departure. Her prayers were answered. She didn't want to suffer or linger in a helpless condition. On Wednesday, she was able to celebrate Mass in the chapel and share in communion. It was her last communion. On Friday morning, the nurse came into the room to prepare her for the start of another day. The nurse stepped out for several minutes. When she returned, the angel of death had claimed Virginia.

There is a prayer card that is frequently passed out at funerals. It includes a prayer by F. Mauriac. In his exalted prose, he states what we are trying to convey at the funeral service:

Grant, Lord, that I lose myself in the peace of Thy presence, so that when my hour comes, I shall pass through a transition almost insensible, from You to You, from You the living bread, the bread of humankind, to You the love alive, already possessed by those of my own beloved, who have gone before me into thy shelter.

Permit me to quote from the Book of Proverbs words that the family and friends of Virginia Nowak could verify.

"Many women have done excellently,
    but you surpass them all."
Charm is deceitful, and beauty is vain,
    but a woman who fears the LORD is to be praised.
Give her a share in the fruit of her hands,
    and let her works praise her in the city gates (31:29–31).

Death of a Husband
Who Adopted Two Sons

First Reading	Is 25:6–9
Responsorial Psalm	Ps 27:1,4,13–14
Second Reading	Rv 21:1–5,6–7
Gospel Acclamation	Rv 14:13
Gospel	Mt 25:31–40

I wish to express my sincere sympathy to Hilda on the death of her dear husband; to their two adopted sons, Gregory and Wendell; and to their grandchildren and friends.

On February 22, the feast day of the Chair of St. Peter, Herman Henry Myers died at the age of eighty-two. Ten hours before he died, he was anointed and conscious enough to share in communion. With his wife, we prayed the Litany of the Saints and the Our Father. Knowing how faithful Herman was, I was reminded of the words of a Miami hospital chaplain, "How could anyone look into the eyes of a dying person and be depressed, when you know within a short time that person will be seeing God face to face."

St. John, in his first letter, vouches for that belief when he writes, "Beloved, we are God's children now; …. What we do know is this: when he is revealed, we will be like him, for we will see him as he is" (1 Jn 3:2). I thought of my own future death as I recited, "Depart, O Christian soul, out of this world, in the name of God, the Father almighty, who created thee; in the name of Jesus Christ, the son of the living God, who suffered and died for thee; in the name of the Holy Spirit, who sanctified thee." Herman had been on the brink of death for over a year. The recurrence of his prostate cancer had spread to other parts of his body. His bones were afflicted, and the pain was great. Heavy doses of pain medication were needed.

Herman's life could not be understood or explained without reference to his faith, which dominated his life. From an early age, he was devoted to the practice of religion. He attended St. Vincent's

41

Prep School, conducted by the Benedictine Order. The school was located in Latrobe, Pennsylvania. He advanced to Duquesne University in Pittsburgh and earned a degree in engineering. He finally found employment in Maryland, with an airplane maintenance company, where he became one of the top executives. The government eventually abandoned the facility and with his contacts, Herman was fortunate enough to become employed by the Department of Energy, where he stayed until his retirement. From early adolescence at St. Vincent's Prep, then at Duquesne University, he never deviated from his religious training. Herman and Hilda did not have children of their own, but they wanted to share their life and good fortune with orphan children. Two boys, Gregory and Wendell, were their choice. Their decision of love, motivated by their faith, completed their purpose in life. Both were accorded a Catholic university education. Herman's motto was based on the truth that educating the mind in the faith of Christ was better than money in the bank.

What are the benefits of serving God? Most people strive to move up the ladder of success in life. No one thinks of this as dysfunctional. In our relationship with God, we strive to climb the ladder of happiness through eternal life with God. The Scriptures endorse such ambitions to encourage believers to persevere.

The first reading from the prophet Isaiah encourages our perseverance in the eternal quest, "God will swallow up death forever. Let us be glad and rejoice in his salvation." Herman led a joyous life. We must celebrate his life with our own joy.

Psalm 27 repeats what is deeply set in every soul that seeks happiness with God, "One thing ... I seek after: to live in the house of the LORD ..., to behold the beauty of the LORD. ... Be strong, and let your heart take courage; wait for the LORD!" There is no comparison between the finite things of earth and the beauty and glory of God.

The theme of Isaiah is very similar to the message of St. John in the last book of the New Testament, the Book of Revelation, and the Greek Apocalypse. "He will wipe every tear from their eyes. Death will be no more; or mourning and crying and pain will be no more, for the first things have passed away." None of us on earth would dare make such promises.

No one will be surprised at the family's selection of the twenty-fifth chapter of St. Matthew's Gospel. It stresses the necessity of good deeds if there is to be sound hope for sharing the gift of life. As often as we hear this selection it pulls us up to the demands and glory of our faith. "Then the king will say to those at his right hand, 'Come, you that are blessed by my Father, inherit the kingdom prepared for you from the foundation of the world .... As you did it to one of the least of these ..., you did it to me."

Herman Henry Myers taught us how to say "good-bye," in the last days of his battle with cancer. He enriched our lives by his generous and kind deeds. He looked forward to his great adventure in heaven and anticipated it with the spirituality that defined his life.

Like his master, he embraced his pain. During this difficult time, Hilda remained by his side. Her husband is irreplaceable. She will be left alone with a feeling of a void in her life. Good people are needed on earth and are sorely missed when they are gone. Through her faith, Hilda will prevail. The loss is only temporary. The day will come when she will be reunited with her husband in heaven. God blessed Hilda with a kind and loving husband. She is grateful to God for granting her fifty-three glorious years with her husband. Could anyone ask for more?

Death of an Elderly Male

First Reading	Eccl 3:1–8,11
Responsorial Psalm	Ps 130:1–2,2–3,4–6,7–8
Second Reading	2 Cor 5:1,6–9
Gospel Acclamation	Mt 11:28
Gospel	Mk 15:33–39

Our sincere sympathy reaches out to the family of Mark Chapin; to his two sons, Richard and Bruce; to his two daughters, Donna and Julie; to the grandchildren; and to relatives and friends.

After breakfast, Mark went out onto the porch to relax and read the morning newspaper in his favorite wicker chair. He closed his eyes and never awoke. His daughter Julie discovered his body. Mark, who was a widower, prayed that he would die a peaceful death, without any lingering agony. Mark's prayer was granted. He passed away at the age of eighty-two.

Coping with the loss of a loved one is never easy, even under what may appear to be the best conditions. The death of an elderly person could be seen as a blessing. When death comes at the twilight of one's life, we are able to accept the death more readily. Our pain and sorrow is eased by knowing the deceased led a very long and full life. Mark was frequently heard saying, "Don't waste your time in grief. I am ready to meet the Lord. Just say a few prayers for me."

The family's strong faith is both a survival tool and a healing tool. Death does hurt. It's part of what St. Paul refers to as "the sting of death." There are no exceptions. It is commonly thought that St. Joseph died before Christ's public ministry. His death was a sad occasion for Mary and her son, Jesus. They found comfort in knowing that Joseph was in the safekeeping of the angels. Death always seems more imminent when we reach old age. The summons can come at any moment. Certainly, Mark was aware of that. A daily regimen of pills, helped to alleviate the aches and pains of old age. He had time to spiritually prepare himself for death. Spurred by his faith, he devoted his time to prayer, especially reciting the rosary. During my visits, he mentioned how many rosaries he recited during the day.

Frequently on his mind was the question of whether it was wrong to pray for death. During my visits to nursing homes and monthly Mass at institutions for the elderly, I have been asked that question many times. When life becomes a burden and the ordinary biological functions a dreadful chore, there is a natural instinct to want to die. Where faith is strong, this occurs quite often. It is understandable that elderly persons may pray for their death. They have lived a long and prosperous life on earth. Sickness and failing health are inevitable in old age. They desire eternal life in heaven with the Lord and loved ones who have passed before them.

The Scripture readings indicate the yearning for God and the grace of heaven as part of our hope for eternal life. A popular quotation from the Book of Ecclesiastes addresses this problem, "A time to be born and a time to die. A time to weep and a time to laugh. A time to mourn and a time to dance. A time to seek and a time to lose. God has made everything suitable for its time." It was Pope John XXIII who stated in his old age, "Any day is a good time to be born and any day is a good time to die."

There is no better palliative than the power of prayer. Praying for death lessens the fear of death. It is a welcome relief and a sign of acceptance. This is the last stage in Elizabeth Kubler-Ross's analysis of dying.

St. Mark emphasized the spiritual agony of Christ upon his crucifixion, "My God, my God, why hast thou forsaken me?" Surely our cross of mortality is far less agonizing.

Movie actor Gary Cooper converted to the Catholic faith. His battle with cancer was bearable because he drew strength in knowing that his Savior Jesus Christ suffered and died for him. St. Paul declares that we are citizens of a lasting city in heaven. Death can be seen as a transition. We must not forget the prayers of repentance and trust found in Psalms 129 and 130. These prayers are traditionally a part of the Christian funeral. When we think of approaching our Savior, a feeling of fear and trembling comes over us. Our fear of the Lord is the beginning of wisdom. Yet this humility and plea for mercy will open the gates of paradise, as it did for the good thief on the cross. The psalm expresses our desperate need for God, "Out of the depths I cry to you, O Lord. Lord, hear my voice! Let your ears be attentive to the voice of my pleading."

William F. Buckley, editor of the *National Review*, wrote an obituary for the father of a close friend (April 1985). The family gathered together and an announcement was made of the death of the elderly man. Several of the younger children who were present absorbed the mood of the family's conversation. As a result, one child seemed to amazingly grasp the meaning of death. This child remarked, "Granddad woke up dead." This is a very appropriate truth, which can be applied to all of us. The greatest theologian couldn't reach the height or depth of that child's observation. What a beautiful way of referring to death as life. Waking up to life in God's home.

Stewart Alsop, along with his brother Joseph, a newspaper columnist, wrote a book entitled *Stay of Execution*. At the time, Stewart was dying of cancer. He wrote, "The dying man needs to die just as the sleeping man needs to sleep. And when that time comes, to resist is not only useless, it is wrong."

Mark Chapin did not resist, but happily accepted the summons of his Creator. He was grateful for his long and happy life and for the love of his daughter, Julie, who cared for him in his old age. May the soul of Mark Chapin, and the souls of all the faithful departed, through the mercy of God, rest in peace.

Death of a Person
Who Committed Suicide

First Reading	Lam 3:17–26
Responsorial Psalm	Ps 27:1,4,10,13,14
Second Reading	Rom 8:14–18
Gospel Acclamation	Jn 11:25,26
Gospel	Lk 23:39–43

I wish to express my sincere condolences to Jane and Bud Brown on the death of their son, Paul; to his brother, Ronald; to his classmates; and to all of his friends.

The community has responded with love and support for the family. Certainly the outpouring of prayers and attention makes the burden a little lighter for the Brown family. On their behalf, I thank you for coming and sharing their sorrow.

There are many avenues by which any one of us may die. The most poignant may be when a loved one makes the choice to end his or her own life. I am sure at some time in our life, when obstacles seem insurmountable, the thought may creep into all of our minds. We rely on faith and tradition to ease our minds regarding salvation.

We express a deep concern for the immortal soul. Two questions may haunt our minds. The first question we ask ourselves is, "Where has my loved one gone?" There is a common theme which runs through most suicide notes, where the person will ask for forgiveness from God and their family. A suicide letter could read, "Tell Mom and Dad that I love them. Don't forget about me. I'm sorry if I made you unhappy. I believe God will understand. I love you all very much. Good-bye."

Will God be forgiving and merciful? The Scripture abounds with unshakable proof that God is always forgiving and merciful, regardless of how or why we die. In such a crisis, strong sympathy springs up in the human soul. Sympathy is the basis of morality. We naturally grant an edge to someone caught in this situation. If parents and friends are so concerned and anxious about salvation, then the Savior Jesus Christ is a thousand times more concerned. God is not cruel. God is a compassionate Father, who desires the salvation of all. "The LORD is my light and my salvation; whom shall I fear?"

God looks at the total life of every person, not just the instantaneous and irrational decisions of the moment. Human nature is weak. Mistakes are made. There occurs at some time a loss of innocence and balance in everyone's life. God understands our depression and his saving power can redeem all actions.

The second question that plagues the minds of family and friends is, "What could I have done to prevent this?" If only I had looked and listened for the cries of help and distress, maybe I could have saved a life. Guilt settles in to haunt the mind and flog the conscience. The poem "For Harry and Joan" by Maisha Jackson asks the same question:

And what about the "what-ifs?"
What if
You hadn't done that, or you had done that
or
I hadn't done that, or I had done this
or
I/We hadn't/had done this or the other?
What about the "what-ifs"?

This is a difficult question to deal with and even more difficult to answer. Grief can be intensified by this nagging guilt, but then again, it seems to be unjustified.

St. Paul's reference to our adoption as children led by the Spirit to cry "Abba! Father!" implies the love and mercy of an unchangeable Savior. *Abba* is an Aramaic word meaning "Daddy." A father would not deny his son his rightful inheritance to the family estate, regardless of any shortcomings. The mere fact of being a son would presuppose the inheritance. So our divine Father, Abba, would not deny an inheritance of glory to any child.

The Gospel of St. Luke accords special treatment for special cases. The cry "Abba! Father!" brings mercy and kindness. The good thief pleads his case for salvation. The Lord, from his throne on the cross, responds, "Today you will be with me in paradise." There is no need to despair with the prayer of "Abba! Father!"

Indeed, suicide is one of the most complicated and heartbreaking tragedies. Permit me to refer to the experience of the television evangelist Oral Roberts, who lost his son, Ronald. In 1982, at the age of thirty-eight, his son shot himself through the heart. His father wrote, "I picked up my Bible and remembered one line about love which 'bears all things.' I found it in Corinthians 13:7. 'Love bears all things, hopes all things, endures all things. Love never fails.' As we read this verse, my family and I cling to it with all the fierceness of faith stronger than ourselves. We still have Ronald ... life must go on and will go on because God's love for us will never fail. Nor will our love for God and for Ronald."

Today our beloved brother Paul, now free of all earthly burdens, has found peace and rest in the arms of a merciful "Abba!"

Death of an Air Disaster Victim

First Reading	Wis 4:7–15
Responsorial Psalm	Ps 27:1,4,7,8,13–14
Second Reading	Rom 5:5–11
Gospel Acclamation	Jn 11:25–26
Gospel	Jn 11:32–45

Our hearts go out in profound sympathy to the parents of Sheila Turner Arnold; to her two brothers, Tom and Harry; to the parents of Keith Arnold; to his sisters, Shirley and Elizabeth; and to the relatives and friends who mourn their loss.

Our little town of less than three thousand population gained the attention of the nation as a result of an air tragedy. As in all major accidents, we had to await the names of the victims, until after the next of kin were notified. Then, the sad announcement was made. Keith and Sheila Arnold along with their two children, Ryan, age twelve, and Shelly, age ten, were victims of a rear wing jet engine explosion, which just before lift-off ripped through the fuselage and instantly killed the family of four.

The Arnold family had visited Sheila's maternal grandparents in Florida. After a happy, enjoyable vacation, rested and anxious to return home, they became victims of a tragic accident. They had no control over the mechanical flaw or possible neglect of maintenance. There is a cliché that quickly comes to mind, "They were situated in the wrong place at the wrong time." Anyone occupying those seats would have been killed instantly. Can anyone anticipate such an eventuality? Accidents happen. It could have happened on the highway near home, or in the kitchen of their house, or anywhere, since danger lurks, we know not where.

All of us feel somewhat diminished and threatened by the speculation about airplane disasters. The flying public is accustomed to one or two major crashes each year; even though, with millions of miles flown, the airlines have a good safety record.

There are no words to express adequately our sadness over this devastating loss. Four innocent people were killed instantly. No pain. No suffering. No warning. No dread of impending death. They died as a family. As the preface of the Mass of Christian burial informs us, "Life is changed, not ended. When the body of our earthly dwelling lies in death, we gain an everlasting dwelling place in heaven."

The Arnold family was close to God through their faith. The Arnold family were not strangers to God. He saw the Arnold family in prayer at Mass. They were baptized and received the gift of adopted children of God and heirs of heaven. They understood the purpose and meaning of their lives as union with God.

The Scripture readings for this morning's Mass help us in our desire to put things in perspective. God can comfort and penetrate our minds and hearts. The liturgy reminds us that what we read and hear has the authority of God. We are reminded of this by our response at the end of the readings, "The Word of the Lord. Thanks be to God."

The first reading, from the Book of Wisdom in the Old Testament, speaks to us of God's goodness, mercy, and compassion. Life isn't always measured in terms of long years or old age. The scale of life varies for each person. These uncertainties are beyond our control. Nevertheless, in all circumstances, though we do not yet understand, "that God's grace and mercy are with his elect and that he watches over his holy ones."

St. Paul's letter to the Romans tells us of the superabundance of justification or salvation. God's love in our hearts is poured forth by the Holy Spirit, who has been given to us. The Holy Spirit activates his power in our souls through prayer, which is the power to transform ourselves and others for salvation. Thus, we are given the virtue of hope. Our prayers for Keith, Sheila, Ryan, and Shelly will be accepted by God, since they are inspired by the Holy Spirit.

The Gospel tells the story of Christ raising Lazarus from the dead. Christ used Lazarus' death for the glory of his Father. Rebuked mildly by Martha for his failure to come and heal Lazarus, Christ uttered the words that reversed the consequences of Adam's fall from grace in the Garden of Eden, "I am the resurrection and the life; whoever believes in me, even if they die, will live, and everyone who lives and believes in me will never die."

Suppose you heard those words for the first time and witnessed the raising of Lazarus after his four days in the tomb. Wouldn't you believe? What happened to Lazarus while dead was of no importance to St. John, though we might be curious: Did Lazarus see and talk to his parents? Did he perceive a radiant light? Did he have an experience of rapture and serenity? What was it like to think and feel without a body?

What is important is faith. Do you believe? My friends, those happy words, "Come forth," spoken to Lazarus, will be spoken to us, as they will be spoken to the Arnold family.

Keith, Sheila, Ryan, and Shelly pledged their faith in Christ, as did Mary and Martha. We pray and commend their souls to God. May God hold them in the palm of his hand. We lean heavily on our faith when we believe that they have left the land of the dying, to go to the land of the living.

Death of a Person with AIDS

First Reading	Dn 12:1–3
Responsorial Psalm	Ps 25:6–7,17–18,20–21
Second Reading	1 Cor 15:51–57
Gospel Acclamation	2 Tm 2:11–12
Gospel	Mt 25:1–13

Our hearts reach out in sincere condolences to Mr. and Mrs. Douglas Fowler on the death of their son Emery; to their two sons, George and Jeffrey; to their daughter, Annabelle; and to all the relatives and friends.

Most of us know that Emery died from AIDS. There has been enough information shown to us in television to alert everyone to the facts of this disease. There is no cure for AIDS. Certainly, it is most fitting at this Mass that we pray for an eventual cure. Also, there is less of a stigma attached to AIDS because of the mass public media service announcements. AIDS is a dreadful disease and anyone afflicted should be treated as any other patient, with the best medical attention and care. They are surely entitled to the spiritual and humane care of the community. We, especially as Christians, must be concerned and involved. AIDS is everyone's problem.

The church has officially announced that AIDS is not to be regarded as a punishment from God. Christianity is not a punitive faith. Rather, as commanded by Christ, we are called to love God and our neighbor as we love ourselves. Emery died at the age of thirty-nine, after fighting the disease for several years. Within the past year, he had returned to his family. His father and mother had convinced him that home was the best place for treatment and care. Hospice provided him with care and comfort for the last couple of months.

During this time, there had been a reconciliation between Emery and his family and friends. After the initial shock of their son's illness, forgiveness and acceptance, without any adverse feelings, united the family. The strong bond of early adolescence was made stronger in this crisis. It gave birth to love and dedication, with a reminder of the reality of what life is all about—faith, love, and compassion as a family.

The pain and suffering of loved ones can teach us the lesson of how to live and how to die. Now, for Emery, there will be no more pain, no more uncertainty. There is only peace. As Scripture puts it, "To set the mind on the Spirit is life and peace" (Rom 8:6). Emery was given the grace of wisdom when he returned and died in the bosom of his family.

As his pastor, I can testify that Emery was prepared to deal with his inevitable fate. There were moments of anger, despair, and denial, which resulted at times with gifts of flowers and plants being thrown in a fit of rage. These moments were always followed by tearful acts of forgiveness and contrition that deepened the love between himself and his family and friends.

Each one of his friends who came to visit him went away with more spirit than what they gave. The capability to watch nature relentlessly sap the strength and vitality from a dying person demands strong faith and prayer to God. Compassion is spontaneous. God accepts us in our helplessness and lack of understanding.

Emery is now at rest. He awaits the second coming of Christ. We shall all arise to hear the trumpet of the Archangel Gabriel, "The hour is coming when all who are in their graves will hear his voice and will come out—those who have done good, to the resurrection of life, and those who have done evil, to the resurrection of condemnation" (Jn 5:28–29). The Scripture readings were selected by Emery. They reflect his gratitude and belief in everlasting life.

I used the word *wise* in reference to the life of Emery. The same word, *wise*, was also read to us in the Gospel. Despite obstacles, Emery acted wisely through his return to his family and to his baptismal faith. The Bible favors the word *wise* to mean acceptance and belief in Christ.

The reading from the Book of Daniel exults over the reward of a wise choice, "Those who are wise shall shine like the brightness of the sky, and those who lead many to righteousness, like the stars forever and ever." To be listed as "wise" radiates to all who are involved in the saving of the soul of a loved one. Therefore, it is possible for life to end with "lived happily ever after." How does this take place? St. Paul uses an observation from nature, the change of a seed to its nonrecognizable new life. The seed must contain what it becomes. Christ plants the seed of eternal life in the souls of those who believe and love him. What happens to a seed? When we plant a seed, it splits and dies. It gives up its nutrients, so that a full, beautiful plant, tree, or flower may spring from it. Such is the case with death. We all must die, so that we may become partakers of the nutrients of eternal life through Christ's resurrection. Thus arises the beautiful transition expressed by St. Paul, "For this perishable body must put on imperishability, and this mortal body must put on immortality. When this perishable body puts on imperishability, and this mortal body puts on immortality, then the saying that is written will be fulfilled: 'Death has been swallowed up in victory.' 'Where, O death, is your victory? Where, O death, is your sting?'"

If you believe the seed contains within itself the power to transform to a new life, then it follows, as St. Paul argues, that mortal life has within itself, the soul, the new life of eternity. Notice again the wise use of the word *must*, both with respect to nature and with respect to a human soul. No person can halt this process.

Chapter 25 of St. Matthew's Gospel gives us a view of the second coming of Christ. The parable that introduces the chapter again uses the word *wise*. The wise are those who prepare and are aware of the reality of life. Oftentimes death sneaks up on us when we least expect it. The parable relates the story of five foolish bridesmaids and five wise ones. The bridegroom was delayed (as we might say) in entering the nuptial banquet. While waiting and sleeping, the wise had the foresight to have an ample supply of oil; the foolish, you might guess, didn't. The unexpected and perverse happened. The bridegroom came and only the wise had the oil for the lamps, to welcome and follow the bridegroom into the wedding feast. The foolish, who were away buying oil, arrived late and received the bad news, "Truly, I tell you, I do not know you."

Lord, welcome into your heavenly banquet your baptized son Emery. You promised that those who followed you shall not die, but have your life. May God's cheerful news be yours forever.

Sudden Death of a Mother

First Reading	Wis 3:1–6,9
Responsorial Psalm	Ps 125 (126)
Second Reading	Rom 6:3–5,8–11
Gospel Acclamation	Jn 12:24
Gospel	Jn 12:23–26

Our hearts go out in sincere sympathy to the family of Helen Conway; to her husband, Ralph; to her sons, David and Gerard; to her daughter, Margaret; to her brothers, James and Raymond; and to her grandchildren, relatives, and friends.

Helen Miller Conway died suddenly, at the age of sixty-six. An ambulance had rushed her to the hospital ER. The hospital staff was unable to save her life. The diagnosis was a stroke caused by cerebral hemorrhaging. Death came scripturally, "like a thief in the night." Her sudden death shocked her family, relatives, and friends.

Helen had been a communion minister and lector who taught for many years in the high school religious education program. She also served as parish chairperson for the Pro-Life Movement.

In his teachings, Christ often used metaphors to explain the mysteries of life, death, and immortality. Someone once said, after the fashion of Archimedes, "Give me a metaphor strong enough and I will move the world." God did move the world, with his gift of eternal life. This gift is enough to dispel all confusion and to calm the minds of all who accept his revelation. Christ declared, "This is eternal life, that they may know you, the only true God, and Jesus Christ whom you have sent" (Jn 17:3).

Christ used the metaphor of the seed planted in the soil when he referred to death as starting a new life and a new beginning. In dying, the seed finds new life. There is no better metaphor to explain death as eternal life; the new life that springs from the seed of death. The acceptance of this metaphor comes out of a rich, deep faith and trust in God.

St. Paul did not flinch from trying to explain the relationship between death and resurrection. He explained the metamorphosis of going from life to immortality with death as the vehicle that makes this possible. Metamorphosis is a law of nature. The best-known example is the caterpillar changing into a beautiful butterfly. The butterfly is the universal symbol of resurrection. With plants, nature provides a metamorphosis every season.

St. John records our Lord's words in his Gospel, "Truly, I tell you, unless a grain of wheat falls into the earth and dies, it remains just a single grain; but if it dies, it bears much fruit. Those who love their life lose it, and those who hate their life in this world will keep it for eternal life." This is a law of nature that nobody can deny. There is a supernatural law that states that a person who dies in Christ will also bear the fruit of immortality.

Christ employs a similar language when referring to eternal life and the kingdom of heaven. Notice the connection with baptism, "Very truly, I tell you, no one can enter the Kingdom of God without being born of water and Spirit" (Jn 3:5). In baptism, we die with Christ and we also rise with Christ. The metamorphosis is from a natural person to a child of God, an heir of heaven. A spiritual change is taking place. We are being transformed by Christ to live in his presence. Through baptism, the seed of eternal life is planted in us. Subsequently, through our death, we bloom into life with God.

The concept of metamorphosis is strong in Christ's teachings. Metamorphosis was mentioned by Christ after he performed the multiplication of five loaves of bread to feed five thousand people "Unless you eat the flesh of the Son of Man and drink His blood, you shall not have life in you" (Jn 6:53). We have no fear of being baptized. We have no fear of consuming the body and blood of Christ. Should we have any fear then, when Christ explains to us that if we die with his seeds of baptism and the Eucharist in us, we will bear his fruit, his life?

Today we celebrate the metamorphosis, the transformation of our sister Helen into a new person clothed with the garment of God's eternal life, the fruit of her love of God. The seed that was planted has died and produced the fruit of immortality.

Death of a Mentally Challenged Daughter

First Reading	Is 49:8–14,16
Responsorial Psalm	Ps 23
Second Reading	Rom 6:3–9
Gospel Acclamation	Lk 18:16
Gospel	Mk 10:13–16

I wish to express my heartfelt condolences to Anthony and Otelia Dolezal on the death of their dear daughter, Agnes; to her brothers, Louis, Joseph, and William; to her sisters, Stephanie and Dorothy; and to her relatives and neighbors.

There are two occasions in our lives when we are inaugurated into an intimate union with Christ. On both occasions, we do not have the capacity to understand the words addressed to us. The first occasion is at our baptism as infants, where we feel the chilly waters and hear the words, but can't understand them. The second occasion is when we are ushered up to the front of the sanctuary at our funeral. In baptism and in death, we cannot speak for ourselves. We depend on our parents and friends.

Agnes Dolezal died at the age of eighteen, from pneumonia. She neither understood, nor could affirm her faith in Christ, her Savior, at baptism. To receive the gift of faith in Christ does not require consent from a baby. Her parents, Anthony and Otelia, gave their consent through the power of giving birth and life to their daughter. Agnes became an adopted daughter of God, with the inheritance of the eternal kingdom. Though she had a physical brain impairment, those gifts were never lost. Her baptismal innocence continued on earth and led her directly to the heavenly kingdom.

Agnes was on the brink of death at birth. She suffered from high fevers and convulsions, which resulted in a severe impairment of her mental faculties and physical ability. She could show affection to her family and awkwardly verbalize the words *Mommy* and *Daddy*, as well as the names of her brothers and sisters.

For eighteen years, she needed constant care and supervision, twenty-four hours a day. Her destiny was to be dependent on the love of her family. Her salvation was the gift of God. She was a blessing and a gift to her family.

Both in life and in death, Agnes belonged to God. Her parish priest asked her family, "Do you believe in God, the Father almighty, Creator of heaven and earth?" They answered, "I do." He asked them, "Do you believe in Jesus Christ, his only Son, Our Lord, who was born of the Virgin Mary, was crucified, died, and was buried, rose from the dead, and is now seated at the right hand of the Father?" They responded, "I do." He asked them, "Do you believe in the Holy Spirit, the holy Catholic Church, the communion of saints, the forgiveness of sins, the resurrection of the body, and life everlasting?" They answered, "I do." Her parish priest and her family gave their consent to this profession of faith, "This is our faith. This is the faith of the church. We are proud to profess it, in Christ Jesus our Lord."

When Anthony and Otelia said their wedding vows, they formed a partnership of faith with God. "Can a woman forget her nursing child, or show no compassion for the child of her womb? Even these may forget, yet I will not forget you. See, I have inscribed you on the palms of my hands." Anthony and Otelia, through their marriage vows, received the grace to give unconditional love to their disabled daughter. In consenting to the commitment and intimacy of marriage, they accepted Agnes as a blessing and a gift of life, regardless of her condition. "In sickness and in health, in good times and in bad, until death do us part." This statement was implicit and understood in their marriage. Agnes belonged to God. She was not a possession of her parents. God was the supernatural parent, who created her soul. God alone has absolute rights over his children. "Know that the LORD is God. It is he that made us, we are his; we are his people, and the sheep of his pasture" (Ps 100:3). While they fulfilled their duty of love, God provided the grace to accept this sacrifice. The result has been great joy rather than an obligation.

The baptismal water, with the words effecting the spiritual adoption, are reflected again as the presider sprinkles the coffin of Agnes at the entrance of the church. "I bless the body of Agnes with the holy water that recalls her baptism, of which St. Paul writes 'All of us who have been baptized into Christ Jesus were baptized into his death. Therefore we have been buried with him by baptism into death, so that, just as Christ was raised from the dead by the glory of the Father, so we too might walk in newness of life. For if we have been united with him in a death like this, we will certainly be united with him in a resurrection like this.'"

Baptism, as St. Paul explains, consists of a ritual dying and rebirth, to a state of incorporation with the divine Savior. This is how it was understood by the early Christians. In this belief, the converts were baptized by the complete submersion of the body in water. Death was represented by the person descending into the deep waters. Ascending or walking out of the water represented the resurrection to life with Christ. The words proclaimed by Christ at the beginning of his public ministry were, "No one can enter the kingdom of God without being born of water and Spirit" (Jn 3:5).

The Dolezal family manifested the power of God's faith and love. Their consolation was fulfilling the will of God, in the care of their innocent child, Agnes. Their reward will be a reunion with Agnes, and their entire family, in Christ's kingdom. On that day, Agnes will be a new creation, no longer disabled, but perfect and beautiful.

Christ has a special love and compassion for children. A culture and civilization will be judged on how it treats its helpless, innocent children. St. Mark preserves Christ's words for our attention. "Let the little children come to me; do not stop them; for it is to such as these that the kingdom of God belongs. Truly I tell you, whoever does not receive the kingdom of God as a little child will never enter it."

We pray for the family of Agnes, that God will strengthen and comfort them in their time of sorrow, until they all meet as a perfect family, in the joyful kingdom prepared by God for those who love and serve him.

Death of an Elderly Widow

First Reading	Eccl 3:1–8,11
Responsorial Psalm	Ps 91(92):2–6,13–16
Second Reading	2 Tim 4:6–8
Gospel Acclamation	Jn 11:25–26
Gospel	Mk 16:1–7

Our sympathies go out to Mrs. Donna Cole on the death of her mother, Dorothy Wescott; to her sons, Albert, Vincent, and Alex; and to the relatives and friends.

Donna and her husband, Leonard, exemplified in a heroic degree, the love and kindness of daily care for an elderly mother. Dorothy Wescott was blessed to have a compassionate daughter and son-in-law. She had expressed her fear of entering a nursing home and being neglected and forgotten. Such fears were allayed by her daughter. Dorothy died at the age of eighty-four from a chronic cardiac vascular disease, at the home of her daughter.

Donna's mother raised and nurtured her for the first eighteen years of her life. She was able to show her gratitude by taking care of her mother for the past ten years. Donna never complained that her life was complicated or confined. Her mother was a widow for many years. She had outlived her close friends. Donna was the last member of her family whom she could rely on. Her brothers lived a long distance away. They usually paid a visit on Dorothy's birthday.

Donna's dedicated care certainly diminished her grief and anxiety near the end. It could be said, by way of consolation, that ten years of constant care was now over. Her mother lived a long life. She was blessed by God. Donna was the agent of God's love for her. Dorothy's troubles are now over, for she died with deep faith in the Lord.

One of the most familiar and frequently quoted passages from the Old Testament is the passage read at this Mass from the book of Ecclesiastes: "For everything there is a season, and a time for every matter under heaven." If you don't believe in heaven, this passage will disappoint you. The author doesn't write "on earth," but "under heaven." The stark reality, which could take a lifetime to ponder, is thrown at us, "a time to be born, and a time to die." This is the story of every person's life. In between birth and death is our decision to be for God or against God. So at this funeral it is "a time to weep, and a time to laugh, a time to mourn, and a time to dance." Thus, we shed tears for our loss and we laugh at the sting of death, which is destroyed by the crucified Christ. While we mourn, we dance in celebration of our loved one returning home to the timeless God. St. Paul vouches for this truth, "O death, where is your sting?"

"A time to be born and a time to die" fits perfectly into a natural analogy of our life. The child growing and developing in the mother's womb is secure, warm, and safe. If the child could reason and communicate, the child might not opt to be born. The child might be afraid of being born into an unknown, hostile, and strange environment. But the child is born.

Once it is cradled in the loving arms of his or her mother or father, the child soon learns that life can be beautiful. The concerned parents will meet their child's needs. The child will quickly accept life with its pleasures and joys.

When death beckons, the body instinctively fights to live. We face a similar situation to that of being in the womb. Although, it is a different kind of womb, the open womb of life. We fear the end of our life on earth. Life, made in the image and likeness of God, can't stop; its nature is to continue, and we have no control over its forces. We can't stop the act of dying. When our soul is forced to leave this dimension of life and enter a new world, an amazing surprise will be waiting for us. Whatever the soul was so fearful of on earth will give way to a greater joy and love in the arms of the heavenly Father. God has made everything suitable for its time, therefore life will no longer depend on time.

Christ chose his own time to be born and his own time to die. St. Mark describes the fearful uncertainties of the holy women on their mission of mercy to complete the anointing of Christ's crucified body. At the sight of the empty tomb, there was a sudden change of heart from fear to joy and belief. They saw and heard the angel's assuring truth, "Do not be alarmed; you are looking for Jesus of Nazareth, who was crucified. He has been raised; he is not here. Look, there is the place they laid him." It was a time for joy and peace.

Dorothy, along with all of us, awaits the good news of the angel at the general resurrection, when the tombs will give up their dead to a new creation of perfection. Until that time, we believe the words of the messenger of God, "Do not be alarmed."

Today, Dorothy says "good-bye" to the darkness of the womb, to childhood, adolescence, middle age, and the golden years; she says "hello" to eternal life.

Appendix A

Homily Desserts

Acceptance of Death

I have always looked forward to death. It would be a terrible prospect, wouldn't it, to just go on and on and on. Everything is bearable because we die .... I have never doubted that our existence in this world has some sort of sequel. It would seem to me preposterous to suppose that this universe was set up solely to provide a *mise-en-scène* for the interminable soap opera of history, with its stock characters and situations endlessly repeated.
  —Malcolm Muggeridge, quoted in *National Review* ([31 December 1990]: 24)

Dying is no big thing, since I'm prepared for it by my Catholic faith.
  —Walker Percy from an interview in *Esquire Magazine*

I know there is a God ... and I see a storm coming; if he has a place for me, I believe that I am ready.
  —John F. Kennedy

Death makes an authentic statement about life's actuality and meaning. It helps clarify and intensify our images of man and his world. Herein lies the summons to advance our comprehension of how death can serve life. To die—this is the human condition; to live decently and die well—this is man's privilege.
  —Herman Feifel, adapted from *A Manual of Death Education* 7

Our institutions have focused upon giving succor to the dying and counseling and comforting the bereaved; but we have shown little concern for the living portion of our lives in relation to death.

No one is mature until he/she has confronted the reality of his/her own death and has ordered his/her life accordingly.
   —Dr. Donald Irish, adapted from A *Manual of Death Education* 48

All praise be yours, my Lord, through sister Death. From whose embrace no mortal can escape. Happy those she finds doing your will.
   —St. Francis of Assisi

I have no property or stocks or insurance. I have no family but a niece and nephew I never see and a brother to whom I am as close as to a mild-mannered short-order cook. I see no friends constantly, only when I'm in the city …. I have no memorabilia, clippings, reviews, photographs, records, printed or manuscript music, I keep only the letters of one man. I refuse to contemplate the past or future. I have no plans, no ambitions or infatuations …. I assume that the worst is likely to occur at any moment and therefore celebrate not so much feeling well as not feeling sick …. Since I have reduced my needs and interests, to a minimum, there will be that much less to die.
   —*The New Yorker*, 12 January 1981 (on the death of one of its staff members, from the published Last Will and Testament)

We must bear hardship in order to ripen. If at times I feel the desire for a life of ease, I go back fondly to a life of hardship, convinced that I learn more from it. This is not the road on which one perishes.
   —Vincent Van Gogh, adapted from A *Manual of Death Education*

When asked at the end of his life if he were prepared to die, Socrates replied: "Know ye that I have been preparing for it all my life."
   —*Bartlett's Familiar Quotations*

Cancer seemed kindly, almost like the preliminary coming of the angel of death to say, "not quite yet. You've time to do some praying and straightening out of life's ledgers." The realization that one has cancer sharpens one's whole view of life; the earth is more beautiful, the sky a little clearer, and every moment of the day precious. God seems to use the things we dread to draw us closer to him. Since we must die and since death is really the entrance into life, I am personally glad that cancer, the kindly messenger, came quite a bit in advance. For life seems sweeter when it melts gently into the life that is eternal promise. God was whispering to me, to get ready to receive your heavenly crown.

—Father Daniel Lord, SJ, from an interview while in the hospital

On the notification of his condition as cancerous, Pope John XXIII reflected: "Well, let God's will be done. Don't worry about me. My bags are packed. I'm ready to go."

Here is a man suffering on his bed of pain, and the church comes to him to perform the sacrament of healing. For this man, as for every person and the whole world, suffering can be the defeat, the way of a complete surrender to darkness, despair and solitude. It can be dying in the very real sense of the word. And yet it can be also the ultimate victory of a person and of life in that person. The church does not come to restore health in this man, simply to replace medicine when medicine has exhausted its own possibilities. The church comes to take this man into the Love and the Life of Christ. It comes not merely to "comfort" him in his sufferings, not to "help" him, but to make him a martyr, a witness to Christ in his very sufferings. A martyr is one who beholds "the heavens opened, and the Son of Man standing on the right hand of God" (Acts 7:56). A martyr is one for whom God is not another—and the last—chance to stop the awful pain; God is his very life, and thus everything in his life comes to God, ascends to the fullness of Love.

—Alexander Schmemann, adapted from A Sourcebook about
  Christian Death 96

Consolation

When death takes someone we love, we die too, and come back to life only through the birth pains of renewal of self, and reaffirmation in God.

    —*Manual of Death Education*

Hospice: to inform patient of death.

    Well, What do you think? And the patient will say, Well, I don't really know. And the nurse will say, Well, what don't you know? So they go back and forth and the patient asks again, Do you think I am dying? And the nurse will say, again, What do you think? And at last the patient might say, Well, I think maybe I am. And the nurse will still not say, Yes, you are. She says, Well, why do you think so? So the patient tells himself.

    —Victor and Rose-Mary Zorza, from *A Way to Die*

Mercy has a human heart. Pity a human face;
and love a human countenance for all the world to see.

    —William Blake

Life in the womb is endowed with qualities that can only achieve their ultimate fulfillment beyond the earth. Why did God endow the child with such unique powers which are only partially realized on earth? God was equipping the child for the supernatural life, with a mind and will to live and exist with the Trinity.

    —Rev. Peter Marshall, Chaplain of the U.S. Congress

Don't torture yourselves about how you feel you may have treated loved ones. Your loved ones understand completely. They are now at peace, and they want you also to be at peace.

    —Cardinal O' Conner, St. Patrick's Cathedral, New York

Mr. Head stood very still and felt the action of mercy touch him again, but this time he knew that there were no words that could name it. He understood that it grew out of agony, which is not denied

to any man and which is given in strange ways to children. He understood it was all a man could carry into death to give his Maker, and he suddenly burned with shame that he had so little of it to take with him. He stood appalled, judging himself with the thoroughness of God, while the action of mercy covered his pride like a flame and consumed it …. He saw that no sin was too monstrous for him to claim as his own, and since God loved in proportion as He forgave, he felt ready at that instant to enter Paradise.
  —Flannery O'Connor, adapted from *A Sourcebook about Christian Death* 111

I am certain that whatever the manner of my death, sudden or foreseen, I shall never lack His mercy.
  —St. Gertrude

Mercy is the fulfillment of justice, not the abolition.
  —St. Thomas Aquinas, from *Summa theologica*, 1,21,3

Reason to rule, but mercy to forgive: The first is law, the last prerogative.
  —John Dryden, from *The Hind and the Panther*

Most of the things of which man is certain, he knows through faith.
  —Seneca

God gave us memories so that we might have roses in December.
  —from a verse on a greeting card

Pope John Paul II put it this way in consoling a person languishing in grief, "You have only one life to live. Jesus says you have two, one here and one in heaven. All of us will rise again. In the idiom of our time, 'you better believe it.'"

The best memorial that we can give a loved one is to live our lives fully. If God were to take away all His blessings, health, physical fitness, intelligence, and leave me but one gift, I would ask for faith—for with faith in Him in His goodness, mercy, love for me, and belief in the everlasting life, I believe I could suffer the loss of my other gifts and still be happy—trustful, leaving all to His inscrutable Providence.

    —Rose Fitzgerald Kennedy, quoted in the *Catholic Standard* ([20 July 1995]: 2)

The act of faith is an act of acceptance, not an explanation.

    —Morris West

All I have seen teaches me to trust the Creator for all I have not seen.

    —Ralph Waldo Emerson

Unless we form the habit of going to the Bible in bright moments as well as in trouble, we cannot fully respond to its consolations, because we lack equilibrium between light and darkness.

    —Helen Keller

This is the comfort of the good, that the grave cannot hold them, and that they live as soon as they die, for death is no more than a turning of us over from time to eternity.

    —William Penn

How can a person be depressed when you look into the eyes of a dying person and know that within a short time that person will see God face to face?

    —Rev. George Goodbout, Miami hospital chaplain, adapted from "When a Loved One Dies" by Betsy Kennedy (*The Voice* [31 May 1985]: 12)

A Catholic priest was called to Calvert Hospital in Washington, D.C., to say some prayers for a woman who was a Buddhist from Thailand: "I took my little prayer book and jar of oil, put the stole on my neck and anointed her on the head and hands. I said the prayers for the dying. It seemed odd to say 'Christian soul' to a Buddhist, but she did not object, and I was sure God could sort things out. Nobody checks ID cards at the pearly gates, no matter what we might once have thought. When I finished the prayers I blessed her, placing my hand on her forehead for a long while, praying silently. I kissed her on the forehead and left her breathing shallowly. 'Go to God,' I said. 'Thank you,' she answered. On the way to the parking lot I wondered why, with more than sixty active clergy in the community, the nurses at a secular hospital sent for a Catholic priest. It seems that almost whenever they need a generic clergyman, they send for me. More important, I think, people feel that Catholics have a ritual for death, one that faces it honestly, without blinking. It says we are dying and need God's mercy. It is a powerful medicine, these last rites. It is a balm in Gilead and a comfort to the dying—even to Buddhists who want a hand across the threshold into eternity."

    —Father Peter Daly, from "Serving As Doorman to Eternity,"
    Catholic Standard ([31 October 1996]: 12)

Death

The greatest day of my life will be the day after they say I'm dead.
    —Daniel Poling

Death is so common within a lifetime families experience frequent stress without any extraordinary help.
    —adapted from *A Manual of Death Education*

No one cheers his own birth, and no one mourns his own death. I am ready to meet my Maker, but whether my maker is prepared for the great ordeal of meeting me is another matter.
    —Winston Churchill

If some died and others did not, death would be a terrible affliction.
    —Jean de La Bruyère

Death has this consolation: it frees us from the thought of death.
    —Jules Renard

Death ought to be our pleasure.
—Tertullian, from *Despectaculis*

There is nothing dreadful in that which delivers from all that is to be dreaded.
—Tertullian, from *Testimony of the Christian Soul*

What is death at most? It is a journey for a season: a sleep longer than usual. If thou fearest death, thou shouldest also fear sleep.
—St. John Chrysostom, from *Homilies*

Death is the separation of soul and body.
—St. Ambrose, from *On the Good of Death*

To the good man to die is gain.
—St. Ambrose, from *De interpell Job*, 2,6

If the death that ends the toil of this life inspires such fear, how greatly that death is to be feared which casts men into everlasting pain!
—St. Augustine, from *Letter*

Of this at least I am certain, that no one has ever died who was not destined to die some time.
—St. Augustine, from *City of God*

For no sooner do we begin to live in this dying body, than we begin to move ceaselessly towards death. For in the whole course of this life (if life we must call it) its mutability tends towards death.
—St. Augustine, from *City of God*

Nothing is more certain than death, nothing more uncertain than its hour.
—St. Anselm, from *Meditations*

Death before death, alive after death.
(*Ante obitum mortuus, post obitum vives.*)
   —Epitaph of St. Francis

Blessed be God for our sister, the death of the body.
   —St. Francis

Death, always cruel, pity's foe in chief. Mother who brought forth grief. Merciless judgment and without appeal!
   —Dante, from *La vita nuova*

Dead as a door nail.
   —William Langland, from *Piers Plowman*

A good death does honor to a whole life.
   —Petrarch, from *Canzoniere*

Against death is worth no medicine.
   —John Lydgate, from *Daunce of Machabree*

God: Where art thou, Death, thou mighty messenger?
Death: Almighty God, I am here at Your will.
   —from *Every Man*

See me safe up: for my coming down, I can shift for myself.
   —St. Thomas More, as he ascended the scaffold

Death makes equal the high and low.
   —John Heywood, from *Be Merry, Friends*

Happy are they who, being always on their guard against death, find themselves always ready to die.
   —St. Francis de Sales, from *Letters to Persons in the World*

What am I who dare to call Thee, God!
And raise my fancy to discourse Thy power?
To whom dust is the period,
Who am not sure to farm this very hour?
For how know I the latest sand
In my frail glass of life, doth not now fall?
And while I thus astonish'd stand
I but prepare for my own funeral?
Death doth with man no order keep;
It reckons not by the expense of years,
But makes the queen and beggar weep.
   —William Habington, from *What Am I Who Dare to Call Thee, God?*

Death quits all scores.
   —James Shirley, from *Cupid and Death*

Death is easier to bear without thought of it than the thought of death without danger.
   —Pascal, from *Pensees*

All human things are subject to decay, And, when fate summons, monarchs must obey.
   —John Dryden, from *Mac Flecknoe*

She vanish'd, we can scarcely say she died.
   —John Dryden, from *Eleonora*

For but a now, did heav'n and earth divide.
   —John Dryden, from *Eleonora*

Devouring famine, plague, and war,
Each able to undo mankind,
Death's servile emissaries are,
Nor to these alone confin'd,
He hath at will
More quaint and subtle ways to kill.
A smile or kiss, as he will use the art,
Shall have the cunning skill to break a heart.
   —James Shirley, from *Cupid and Death*

These death-seal'd lips are they dare give the lie
To the loud boasts of poor mortality;
These curtain'd windows, this retired eye
Outstares the lids of large-look'd tyranny.
This posture is the brave one this that lies
Thus low, stands up (methinks) thus, and defies
The world. All-daring dust and ashes!
only you
Of all interpreters read nature true.
   —Richard Crashaw, from *Death's Lecture at the Funeral of a Young
     Gentleman*

I wish to have no wishes left,
But to leave all to Thee:
And yet I wish that Thou shouldst will
Things that I wish should be.
And these two wills I feel within,
As on my death I muse:
But, Lord! I have a death to die,
And not a death to choose.
   —Frederick Faber, from *Wishes about Death*

The silver chord in twain is snapp'd
The golden bowl is broken,
The mortal mould in darkness wrapp'd
The words funereal spoken;
The tomb is built, or the rock is cleft,
Or delved is the grassy clod,
And what for mourning man is left:
O what is left—but God!
   —Anonymous, from *God and Heaven*

Whilst I dwell, O my God, in this valley of tears,
For refuge and comfort I fly unto Thee;
And when death's awful hour with its terrors appears,
O merciful Jesus, have mercy on me.
   —W. Young, from *Bona Mors*

When I am lying cold and dead,
With waxen taper at my head,
The night before my mass is said;
And friends that never saw my soul
Sit by my catafalque to dole
And all my life's good deeds unroll;
O Jesu, Jesu, will it be
That Thou wilt turn away from me?
   —Hugh Francis Blunt, from *What No Man Knoweth*

She lay asleep. We could not think her dead.
The vivid spirit never knew eclipse.
The angel's kiss that loosed her prison gates
Had left a happy smile upon her lips.
Age, pain, and care fell from her like a sheath
That burst its bond to set the flower free,
And on the quiet brow we saw instead
The bloom of joyous immortality.
   —Sister M. Angelita, from *The Quiet Heart*

Death is no foeman, we were born together;
He dwells between the places of my breath,
Night vigil at my heart he keeps and whether
I sleep or no, he never slumbereth.
Though I do fear thee, knight of the sable feather,
Thou wilt not slay me, death!
   —Sister Madeleva, from *Knights Errant*

Death reduces man to nothing, and it is only tolerable if a man has already faced and accepted his nothingness. The man who has accepted his own nothingness has already absorbed his own death. But in doing this he has already awakened to a light that is immortal and eternal, for it is only by participation in this light that a man can see his own nothingness clearly—the empiricist mind, the calculative intellect, is completely incapable of this vision.
   —Noel O' Donoghue, from *Heaven in Ordinarie*

The greater the love, the more false to its object,
Not to be born is the best for man;
After the kiss comes the impulse to throttle,
Break the embraces, dance while you can.
   —Wystan Hugh Auden

My child asked me "what is a funeral?"
I told him it's when someone dies and everyone
Who loved him comes together to say ...
We love you and we're sorry you couldn't stay with us.
   —adapted from a poem entitled "For Harry and Joan"
      by Maisha Jackson

Because I could not stop for Death,
He kindly stopped for me—
The Carriage held but just Ourselves
And Immortality.
   —Emily Dickinson

Death be not proud, though some have called thee
Mighty and dreadful, for thou art not so,
For those whom thou thinks't thou dost overthrow,
Die not, poor death, nor yet canst thou kill me.
   —John Donne

Fortinbras, upon discovering Hamlet dead, exclaims, "O proud death!" (act V, scene 2). Death is powerful, we seem so powerless against it. Even Hamlet, noble in character and a prince, succumbs.

All say, "How hard it is that we have to die"—A strange complaint to come from the mouths of people who have had to live.
   —Mark Twain

Death, the only immortal who treats us all alike, whose pity and peace and whose refuge are for all—the soiled and the pure, the rich and the poor, the loved and the unloved.
   —Mark Twain

Each person is born to one possession which out values all his others—his last breath.
   —Mark Twain

In answer to the question as to what sort of death was the best, Caesar replied, "A sudden death."

Pity is for the living, envy for the dead.
   —Mark Twain

The beautiful pine casket in which Dorothy Day's body lay during the 1980 wake at Maryhouse, the funeral at the Nativity Church around the corner and burial on Staten Island was so strikingly apt that it shocked one into consciousness of the incongruity of most coffins. It served so aptly the plain simplicity, grace, discernment, insight, honesty, directness, dignity of that great woman's remarkable life and ministry. The body was the sign, not the casket, and yet the casket communicated a craft and showed a care befitting its servant role.

—Robert Hovda, from *A Sourcebook about Christian Death* 80

"When Christ calls a man," writes Bonhoeffer, "He bids him come and die." This dying does not consist in some mystical experience nor is it to be regarded as a mere passivity. It is principally in the genuine love and service of others that we die to ourselves and in active resignation to the demands arising therefrom.

—Andrew O'Donohue, from *Death and Resurrection*

Formerly, they used to bring food to the house of mourning. The rich in baskets of gold and silver, the poor in baskets of willow twigs; and the poor felt ashamed. Therefore, a law was instituted that all should use baskets of willow twigs. Formerly they used to bring out the deceased for burial, the rich on a tall state bed, ornamented and covered with rich coverlets, the poor on a plain bier (or box); and the poor felt ashamed. Therefore, a law was instituted that all should be brought out on a plain bier ... Formerly the expense of the burial was harder to bear by the family than the death itself, so that sometimes they fled to escape the expense. This was so until Rabban Gamaliel insisted that he be buried in a plain linen shroud instead of costly garments. And since then we follow the principle of burial in a simple manner.

—Talmud, quoted in *A Sourcebook about Christian Death* 38

Close your eyes and picture your own death. Your first reaction may be somewhat akin to touching a live cobra. It may also seem disquieting and morbid. But according to Father George Goodbout, a health care expert and nationally acclaimed counselor to dying patients, this is a healthy exercise in preparing yourself for the inevitable death experience. You can't learn to accept a loved one's death until you learn to accept your own.

>—Rev. George Goodbout, Miami hospital chaplain, adapted from "When a Loved One Dies" by Betsy Kennedy (*The Voice* [31 May 1985]: 12)

Fear of Death

It is a poor thing for anyone to fear that which is inevitable.

>—Tertullian, from *The Testimony of the Christian Soul*

For it is for him to fear death who is not willing to go to Christ. It is for him to be unwilling to go to Christ who does not believe that he is about to reign with Christ.

>—St. Cyprian, from *On Immortality*

For man is by nature afraid of death and of the dissolution of the body; but there is the most startling fact, that he who has put on the faith of the Cross despises even what is naturally fearful, and for Christ's sake is not afraid of death.

>—St. Anthanasius, from *On the Incarnation of the Word of God*

The foolish fear death as the greatest of evils, the wise desire it as a rest after labors and the end of life.

>—St. Ambrose, from *On the Good of Death*

If we fear death before it comes, we shall conquer it when it comes.

>—Pope St. Gregory I, from *Homilies on the Gospels*

Sudden death is the only thing to dread, that is why confessors dwell with the great.

>—Pascal, from *Pensees*

From a sudden and unprovided death, deliver us, O Lord.
—adapted from Litany of the Saints

Why fear thee, brother death,
That sharest, breath by breath,
This brimming life of mine?
Each draught that I resign
Into thy chalice flows.
Comrades of old are we;
All that the present knows
Is but a shade of me:
My self to thee alone
And to the past is known.
—J. B. Tabb, adapted from *My Messmate*

Death, the late Professor R. C. Zaehner wrote, is God's gift to man, a gift we should accept not in fear and trembling, but in joy, for we have the assurance, not only in Christianity but in all great religions, that what we call death is nothing more than the break-up of the husk of self-love and the release within us of the sap of a selfless love which is both human and divine, the Holy Spirit who dwells in the hearts of all.
—quoted by Cardinal Hume, OSB, in *Searching for God*

At the beginning of the Second World War, while the bombs were beginning to rain upon London, King George IV of Great Britain went on the air with his annual Christmas Broadcast, and quoted the first five lines of a little-known poem by a little-known English poet, M. Louise Haskins:

And I said to the man who stood at the gate of the year:
"Give me a light that I may tread safely into the known!"
And he replied,
"Go out into the darkness and put your hand into the hand of God.
That shall be to you better than light and safer than a known way."

Dying is no big deal. The least of us will manage that. Living is the trick.
—Red Smith

In his Pulitzer prize winning book, *The Denial of Death*, Ernest Becker says: "… the idea of death, the fear of it, haunts the human animal like nothing else; it is a main spring of human activity—activity designed largely to avoid the fatality of death, to overcome it by denying in some way that it is the final destiny for man."
—quoted by William A. Berry, SJ, in *America* ([28 November 1987]: 409)

People living deeply have no fear of death.
—Anaïs Nin

No evil can happen to a good man, either in life or after death. The hour of departure has arrived, and we go our way—I to die, and you to live, which is better God only knows.
—Plato

Denial of God

Nobody talks so constantly about God as those who insist that there is no God.
—Heywood Braun

God comprehends even the atheism of the atheist.
—Gandhi

An atheist is a man who does not believe in God and wants others to share his belief.

An atheist cannot find God for the same reason a thief cannot find a policeman.

An atheist is a man who can take any text in the Bible and prove that it doesn't mean what is says.

No man hates God without first hating himself.
—Bishop Fulton J. Sheen, from *Peace of Soul*

Men will be ruled by God or by tyrants.
—William Penn

There are no atheists in the foxholes.
—William Thomas Cummings in a field sermon in Bataan
(from *I Saw the Fall of the Philippines* [1942])

Agnosticism solves not, but merely shelves the mysteries of life. When agnosticism has done its withering work in the mind of man, the mysteries remain as before; All that has been added to them is a settled despair.
—V. McNabb, from *Thoughts Twice-dyed*

If God didn't exist, man would invent One.
—Voltaire

The chief function of agnosticism is to awake men from the dogmatic slumber of denial.
—V. McNabb, from *Thoughts Twice-dyed*

There are two kinds of atheists: those who think they are atheists, and those who are atheists.
—J. Maritain, from *Range of Reason*

The exile of God means the tyrannization of man.
—Bishop Fulton J. Sheen, from *Life Is Worth Living*

The fool has said in his heart: There is no God above (Ps 13). The "fool" in the Bible is not an ignoramus; nor is he a theoretical atheist or agnostic, a phenomenon apparently unknown to the Old Testament writers living in a polytheistic world. He is one who has his values all

wrong and is encouraged by past experience to behave as if God would never take action.
  —from *The Psalms* (Paulist Press, 1968), new translation,
    in reference to Psalm 13

Agnosticism leads inevitably to moral indifference. It denies us all power to esteem or to understand moral values, because it severs our spiritual contact with God who alone is the source of all morality and who alone can punish the violation of moral laws with a sanction worthy of our attention.
  —Thomas Merton, from *The Ascent to Truth*

There are but two ways, the way to Rome and the way to atheism.
  —Cardinal Newman, from *Apologia pro Vita Sua*

If God exists, all things are possible; if God does not exist, all things are permissible.
  —Dostoyevsky

A man has to put his trust in something in order to live at all. What you put your final trust in is God. The answer which Martin Luther gave to the question what it means to have a God, or what is God, was that what you hang your heart on and confide in is your God. It may be gold, it may be power, it may be nationalism or a classless society. It may be democracy or science. But in every instance there is the last resort on which a man depends and to which he gives his final allegiance. In this sense it may be maintained that a man cannot be an atheist.
  —J. H. Oldman, quoted in *He Died As He Lived* by Donald B.
    Strobe

An atheist is a person who believes himself an accident.
  —F. Thompson

Devil

May you be dead a half hour before the devil finds out.
—Irish Proverb

The devil comes and tempts all the servants of God. Those who are strong in the faith resist him and he goes away from them, because he cannot find entrance. So, he goes then to the empty and, finding an entrance, he goes into them. Thus he accomplishes in them whatever he pleases and makes them his slaves.
—Shepherd of Hermas, adapted from *Mandate*

Regarding the devil and his angels, and the opposing influences, the teaching of the Church has laid down that these beings exist indeed; but what they are, or how they exist, it has not explained with sufficient clearness. This opinion, however, is held by most, that the devil was an angel, and that having become an apostate he induced as many of the angels as possible to fall away with himself, and these up to the present time are called his angels.
—Origen, adapted from *De principiis, Proem.* 6

In all God's universe there is one, and only one, creature whom we know positively to be damned. And that creature is the devil. But remember, my dear young friends, though the devil is damned, he is no damn fool.
—J. B. Tabb, adapted from *Litz, Father Tabb*

Ours is a world where people don't know what they want and are willing to go through hell to get it.
—Don Marquis

Each of us bears his own hell.
—Virgil

The Devil hath not, in all his quiver's choice,
An arrow for the heart like a sweet voice.
Polygamy may well be held in dread,
Not only as a sin, but as a bore.
  —Lord Byron

Satan fell by the force of gravity: he took himself too seriously.
  —G. K. Chesterton

In all systems of theology the devil figures as a male person.
  —Don Marquis

Satan never takes a vacation, probably because he's accustomed to the heat.

The devil never sleeps.

Satan hasn't a single salaried helper; the opposition employs a million.
  —Mark Twain

The devil is a gentleman who never goes where he is not welcome.
  —John A. Lincoln

The devil can cite scripture for his purpose.
  —William Shakespeare

The devil hath power to assume a pleasing shape.
  —William Shakespeare

Disbelief

On the *David Letterman Show*, Gordon Liddy was asked this question, "What does the future hold for you?" He replied, "The same as for you in the grand scheme of things—we shall provide a diet for the worms."

The thinking of nonbelievers was reflected in the Sunday, June 31, 1994, *New York Times* magazine section with an alleged Soviet spy, Felix Bloch. He had worked for the State Department in Vienna, Austria, where he was born. Bloch confided his gloomy philosophy, "We all die separately. Very few grieve for us, and even those who grieve soon forget us. And those who don't are gone fairly soon anyway. As they say, 'Life is a bitch, and then you die.' Then oblivion. I think that's what I'll get when I die. Oblivion."

The end of it is dreary, the middle is worthless, and the commencement is ridiculous ... I wish I had never been born.
　—Voltaire, quoted in *You Cannot Hold Back the Dawn* by Rev. John C. Dowd

What is the worst of the woes that sat on age to view each loved one blotted from life's page, and be alone, as I am now.
　—Lord Byron

Life's but a walking shadow, a poor player that struts his hour upon the stage. And then is heard no more; it is a tale, told by an idiot, full of sound and fury signifying nothing.
　—William Shakespeare, adapted from *Macbeth*

He sits, this man, and asks me how I want the twins buried. I am not religious, and I cannot bear the religious smell of the funeral home, the flowers, the unctuous voices, the false comfort. Dead is dead. To put a name on plaques, to say prayers—all this is lies, bullshit in the face of the nothingness of death. And in believing this I am at one with my wife, who, even as we met with the funeral parlor man, is taking the first of the pills that will dry up the painful milk that has come to feed the dead babies we are discussing.
　—adapted from "Talk of the Town," *New Yorker*

What will you do, God, if I die?
I am your jug, what if I shatter?
I am your drink, what if I spoil?
I am your robe and your profession
Losing me, you lose your meaning.
　　—Rilke, adapted from *Existential Psychotherapy*

Do not delude yourself with lies,
Like the beast man simply dies,
and after that comes nothing.
　　—Playwright Bertoli Brecht of the "Threepenny Opera"

The worm, the canker, and the grief are mine alone.
—Lord Byron

Funeral Eulogies

A funeral eulogy is a belated plea for the defense delivered after the evidence is all in.
　　—Irvin S. Cobb

I did not attend his funeral, but I wrote a nice letter saying I approved it.
　　—Mark Twain

We usually meet all our relatives only at funerals where someone always observes, "Too bad we can't get together more often."
　　—Sam Levenson

Some men never head a procession until they are dead.
　　—Mark Twain

No matter how famous a man is, the size of his funeral depends partly on the weather.
　　—Mark Twain

Satire lies about literary men while they live; and eulogy lies about them when they die.

Few sinners are saved after the first twenty minutes of a sermon.
—Mark Twain

Americans are so tense and keyed up that it is impossible even to put them to sleep with a sermon.
—Norman Vincent Peale

Death is the only time people will listen attentively to a person being praised.
—R. C. Sonefeld

Somewhere over Greenland in mid September, His Eminence showed me his funeral plans. I began to cry. I saw things that he had listed. I saw my name. I saw the name of Cardinal Mahony, whom he asked to celebrate this Mass of Christian Burial, I saw the name of another close good friend, Father Donohue, whom he asked to deliver the homily at the prayer service for priests. As I cried, he said, "Don't worry, I have cried, too."
—Rev. Msgr. Kenneth Velo, from the November 20, 1996, homily of the funeral Mass of Cardinal Joseph Bernardin

Grief

Grief is not an illness. It is a normal lifetime experience, a process that needs to be dealt with. The process of accommodation is different for everyone.
—Dr. Phyllis Silverman, Harvard Medical School

People say, "Time heals," yet time by itself doesn't heal. If a person in grief sits in a corner waiting for time to heal, to take care of bitter sorrow, time won't do anything. It is what we do with time that can heal.
—Rev. Arnaldo Pangrazzi

In this sad world of ours, sorrow comes to all, and it often comes with bitter agony. Relief is not possible except with time. You cannot now believe that you will ever feel better. But this is not true. You are sure to be happy again. Knowing this, truly believing it, will make you less miserable now.
—Abraham Lincoln

You must not grieve too much. God almighty can set it right.
—R. H. Benson, from *The King's Achievement*

All those who try to go it alone,
Too proud to be beholden for relief,
Are absolutely sure to come to grief.
—Robert Frost, from *Haec Fabula Docet*

Grief and death were born of sin and devour sin.
—St. John Chrysostom, from *Homily*

Take sorrow out of your heart, for it is the sister of divided purpose and violent anger.
—Shepherd of Hermas, from *Mandate*

And where was I to find such pleasures save in you, O Lord, You who use sorrow to teach, and wound us to heal, and kill us lest we die to you.
—St. Augustine, from *Confessions*

Earth hath no sorrow that heaven cannot heal.
—Thomas More, from *Come, Ye Disconsolate*

Where there is sorrow, there is holy ground.
—Oscar Wilde, from *De Profundis*

Nothing can make up for the absence of someone we love, and it would be wrong to try to find a substitute; we must simply hold out and see it through. That sounds very hard at first, but at the same time it is a great consolation, for the gap, as long as it remains unfilled,

preserves the bonds between us. It is nonsense to say that God fills the gap; God doesn't fill it, but on the contrary, keeps it empty and so helps us to keep alive our former communion with each other, even at the cost of pain.
—Dietrich Bonhoeffer

A man's dying is more the survivors' affair than his own.
—Thomas Mann, from *The Magic Mountain*

What we call mourning for our dead is perhaps not so much grief at not being able to call them back as it is grief at not being able to want to do so.
—Thomas Mann, from *The Magic Mountain*

Grief can take care of itself, but to get the full value of a joy you must have somebody to divide it with.
—Mark Twain

Why is it that we rejoice at a birth and grieve at a funeral? It is because we are not the person involved.
—Mark Twain

Men we are, and must grieve when the shades of that which once was great is passed away.
—William Wordsworth

Nothing begins, and nothing ends,
That is not paid with moan;
For we are born in other's pain,
And perish in our own.
—F. Thompson, adapted from *Daisy*

O do not believe that sheer suffering teaches. If suffering alone taught, all the world would be wise, since everyone suffers. To suffering must be added mourning, understanding, patience, love, openness and the willingness to remain vulnerable.

   —Anne Morrow Lindbergh, adapted from *God's Response to Untimely Death*

Out of every tragedy can come a blessing or a curse, compassion or bitterness—the choice is yours.

   —Dr. Elizabeth Kubler-Ross

Heaven

An elderly missionary couple were returning from a life of foreign service. On the same boat, the President of the United States and his party were also arriving from a foreign tour. Great crowds of people greeted the President. There was no one there to greet the missionary and his wife. Later in their hotel room, the old missionary grieved to his wife, "We spent our lives on a foreign field and no one was there to greet us when we came home." The thoughtful wife answered, "But, Darling, we aren't home yet."

Heaven would be hell to an irreligious man.

   —Cardinal Newman, adapted from *Miscellanies*

In his spiritual testament Pope John XXIII wrote, "Oh, what a fine band of souls awaits us and prays for us! I think of them all the time. To remember them in prayer gives me courage and joy, in the confident hope of joining them in the everlasting glory of heaven!" Nearly everyone is in favor of going to heaven, but too many are hoping they'll live long enough to see an easing of the requirements.

"Lord, it's been a wild and crazy vacation, but it's nice to be back home in heaven."
—Msgr. Hugh Michael Beahan, quoted in *St. Mary's Seminary Bulletin*

I would love God even though heaven and hell didn't exist.
—St. Therese of the Little Flower

All the way to heaven is heaven.
—St. Gertrude

I'm a pilgrim in the journey looking for home, and Jesus told me the Church is my home, and Jesus told me that heaven is my home and I have here no lasting city. Cardinals, Archbishops, Bishops: My brothers, Oh Church, please help me to get home.
—Sister Thea Bowman

Let us observe, how the ruler is continually displaying the resurrection that will be, of which God made the first fruits in raising the Lord Jesus Christ from the dead. Let us look, Beloved, at the resurrection which happens regularly. Day and night show us a resurrection; the night goes to sleep, the day rises; the day departs, night comes on. Let us take the crops. How does the sowing happen, and in what way? "The sower went out" and cast each of the seeds into the ground. These fall dry and bare on the ground and decay. Then from the decay the mightiness of the Ruler's providence raises them up, and may grow from the one and bear fruit.
—Clement of Rome

The attempt to externalize the kingdom of heaven in temporal shape must end in disaster. Those who seek it alone will reach it together, but those who seek it in company will perish by themselves.
—Malcolm Muggeridge

Heaven has no rage like love to hate turned, nor hell a fury like a woman scorned.

—William Congreve

Good-bye, proud world; I'm going home;
Thou are not my friend and I'm not thine.

—Ralph Waldo Emerson, adapted from *Good-bye*

Wherein lies happiness? In that which becks
Our ready minds to fellowship divine,
A fellowship with essence; till we shine,
Full alchemized, and free of space. Behold
The clear religion of heaven!

—John Keats, adapted from *Endymion*

The bottom line is in heaven.

—Edwin Herbert Land

If I cannot bend Heaven, I shall move Hell.

—Virgil

No ascent is too steep for mortals. Heaven itself we seek in our folly.

—Virgil

Thou hast made us for Thyself, O Lord, and our hearts are restless until they rest in Thee.

—St. Augustine, from *Confessions*

The surprising thing about heaven is that it remains a heaven with so many different women living under the same roof. It could happen only in heaven.

—Ed Howe

What a pity that the only way to heaven is in a hearse.

—Stanislaw J. Lec

You cannot enter the kingdom of God without election, subjection, and inspection; otherwise it's rejection.

There will be lots of people in heaven just as surprised to see you there as you will be to see them.

Many might go to heaven with half the labor they go to hell.
—Ben Johnson

The wicked often work harder to go to hell than the righteous do to enter heaven.
—Josh Billings

One of the pleasures of heaven must be reading the weather reports from hell.

The Difference between heaven and hell is our love of God.

On earth there is no heaven, but there are pieces of it.
—Jules Renard

Holy Humor

How would the preacher deal with the death of Noah in Genesis who lived 950 years? Tommy DiNardo, the Catholic Christian comedian, has the answer. "Noah built the ark, but it took him 100 years. Apparently it was a government project. What do you say to someone who is 950 years old? Noah, you don't look a day over 800, man! It's that fat-free diet, isn't it? And what do you say at the guy's funeral? Finally!?"
—Diocese of Cleveland's *Catholic Universe Bulletin*
(8 March 1996)

If heaven is not real, I shall be madder than hell.
—Father Walter Burghardt, SJ (*Catholic Standard* [28 March 1996]: 32)

When I am dead, I hope it may be said, "His sins were as scarlet, but his books were read."
—Hilaire Belloc

Malcolm Lowry
Late of the Bowery
His prose was flowery
And often glowery
He lived, nightly, and drank, daily,
And died playing the ukelele.
—Malcolm Lowry

Death and taxes and childbirth: there's never any convenient time for any of them.
—Margaret Mitchell

Few things are harder to put up with than the annoyance of a good example.
—Mark Twain

Thank God, I'm an atheist.
—Mark Twain

Ireland is 95% Catholic. Yet Ireland is very tolerant of atheists. They even have a dial-a-prayer for atheists. You dial the number and nobody answers.
—*The Furrow*

Adam was but human—This explains it all. He did not want the apple for the apple's sake, he wanted it only because it was forbidden.
—Mark Twain

As out of place as a Presbyterian in hell.
—Mark Twain

Depressions may bring people closer to church, but so do funerals.
—Clarence Darrow

Why do they put the Gideon Bibles only in the bedrooms, where it's usually too late, and not in the bar room downstairs?
—Christopher Morley

I know I have to die. I just don't want to be around when it happens.
—Woody Allen

A clergyman is a man who undertakes the management of our spiritual affairs as a method of bettering his temporal ones.
—Bierce Ambrose

Young man, sit down, and keep still; You will have plenty of chances yet to make a fool of yourself before you die.
—Josh Billings

Life is short, but it is long enough to ruin any man who wants to be ruined.
—Josh Billings

We all labor against our own cure, for death is the cure of all diseases.
—Thomas Browne

The dead being the majority, it is natural that we should have more friends among them than among the living.
—Samuel Butler

If I were to be hanged in an open square in London, I would have a larger audience than if I delivered an important speech from the King's castle balcony.
—Winston Churchill

Suicide is the worst form of murder, because it leaves no opportunity for repentance.
—John C. Collins

Here lies my wife. Here let her lie. Now she's at peace and so am I.
—John Dryden

How easy it is for a man to die rich, if he will but be contented to live miserable.
—Henry Fielding

Time is a circus that is always packing up and moving away.
—Ben Hecht

Death: to stop sinning suddenly.
—Elbert Hubbard

Life is a predicament which precedes death.
—Henry James

When Buster Keaton was asked why he kept a deck of cards and a rosary in his pocket, he responded, "When I die, I'll be prepared for either place."

It has been my experience that folks who have no vices have very few virtues.
—Abraham Lincoln

Marriage is neither heaven nor hell; it is simply purgatory.
—Abraham Lincoln

A cynic is a man who, when he smells flowers, looks around for a coffin.
—H. L. Mencken

Man weeps to think that he will die too soon; woman, that she was born so long ago.
—H. L. Mencken

Some ministers would make good martyrs; they are so dry they would burn well.
—Charles H. Spurgeon

Heaven goes by favor; if it went by merit, you would stay out and your dog would go in.
—Mark Twain

The reports of my death are greatly exaggerated.
—Mark Twain

Humorous Stories

A clergyman awoke one morning to find a dead donkey in his front yard after the parish had a living nativity scene several days before Christmas. He had no idea how it got there, but he knew he had to get rid of it. So he called the sanitation department, the health department and several other agencies. But no one seemed to be able to help him. In desperation, the good Reverend called the Mayor and asked what could be done. The Mayor must have been having a bad day. "Why bother me?" he asked. "You're a clergyman. It's your job to bury the dead." The pastor lost his cool. "Yes," he snapped, "but I thought I should at least notify the next of kin."
—Tom Wild Martinez, *The Augusta Chronicle*

Did you hear the story about the man that read the obituary column in the newspaper the first thing when he got up. And his wife asked him, "Why in the world do you rush out and get the newspaper and read the obituary column first, even before you eat breakfast?" And he smiled and said, "Well, honey, I read it to make sure my name's not in it—and then I breathe a sigh of relief and go on and enjoy the day."
—Roger Lovette, from *Writing Your Own Obituary*

"You poor dear, it's too bad he's gone," consoled Bertha to the widow of a man who drowned, "I hope you were left with something." "Oh, I was!" assured the widow. "He left me 100,000."

"A hundred thousand! Imagine that! And him that couldn't read or write." The widow nodded her head. "Or swim," she added.

Hugh Burnett, television producer for the British Broadcasting Corporation, decided he needed some professional help in preparing two satirical programs, one on "heaven" and the other on "hell." He wrote to Father Angelus Andrew, OFM, BBC's Catholic consultant, asking how he could get the official Catholic view of "heaven" and "hell." The memorandum he got back consisted of one word. "Die."

There are three things which are real: God, human folly and laughter. The first two are beyond our comprehension. So we must do what we can with the third.

 —John F. Kennedy (Some of his friends suggested that these
  lines which he had inscribed on a silver beer mug might well
  serve as his epitaph.)

Immortality

We maintain that after life has passed away thou still remainest in existence, and lookest forward to a day of judgment, and according to thy desserts art assigned to misery or bliss.

 —Tertullian, from *The Soul's Testimony*

Who at this day is without the desire that he may be often remembered when he is dead? Who does not give all endeavor to preserve his name by works of literature, or by the simple glory of his virtues, or by the splendor even of his tomb? How is it the nature of the soul to have these posthumous ambitions and with such amazing effort to prepare the things it can only use after decease? It would care nothing about the future, if the future were quite unknown to it?

 —Tertullian, from *The Soul's Testimony*

After the royal throne comes death; after the dunghill comes the Kingdom of Heaven.
—St. John Chrysostom, from *Homilies*

The immortality of the soul is a matter which concerns us so strongly, which touches us so closely, that a man must have lost all feeling not to care to know about it. All our acts and thoughts must follow such different lines, according as there is or is not eternal bliss to look for. That no step can be taken with sense and judgment unless we keep our eyes steadily fixed on this point which must be our final aim.
—Pascal, adapted from *Pensees*

And doom'd to death, though fated not to die.
—Dryden, from *The Hind and the Panther*

The world cannot reconcile itself to the silence of the grave; it is haunted, and in idle moments when it is taken off its guard it shows itself thoroughly committed to some kind of belief in an after-life.
—M. C. D'Arcy, adapted from *Death and Life*

Immortality is not a more or less precarious, successful or unsuccessful survival in other men, or in the ideal waves of the universe. Immortality is a nature-given, inalienable property of the human soul as a spiritual substance. And grace makes eternal life possible to all, to the most destitute as well as to the most gifted.
—J. Maritain, adapted from *Range of Reason*

I danced on a Friday when the sun turned black;
It's hard to dance with the devil on your back;
They buried my body, and they thought I'd gone;
But I am the dance, and I still go on.
—Sydney Carter

This world is not conclusion;
A sequel stands beyond,
Invisible as music,

But positive, as sound.
 —Emily Dickinson

The blazing evidence of immortality is our dissatisfaction with any other solution.
 —Ralph Waldo Emerson

Everyone wants the eternal life but damn few people are willing to give up what they have to get it.
 —Jim Jones, author of *From Here to Eternity*

Without confidence in immortality one actually believes in nothing.
 —Dostoyevsky

But at my back I always hear
Time's winged chariot hurrying near.
And yonder all before my life
Deserts of vast eternity.
 —Andrew Marvell, adapted from *To His Coy Mistress*

The morning drum-call on my eager ear
Thrills unforgotten yet; The morning dew
Lies yet undried along my field of noon.
But now I pause at whiles in what I do,
And count the bell, and tremble lest I hear
(My work untrimmed) the sunset gone too soon.
 —Robert Louis Stevenson

Time is short, eternity is long.
 —Cardinal Newman, from *Development of Christian Doctrine*

So must outlive we even earth and sky,
Thou, O God, and I, in one persistent now.
And when eternity is old then Thou
Shalt still be young, but how much younger I!
 —Edwin Essex, adapted from *Epigram*

"A good point to underscore this early in a New Year," writes Martin Duggan in the *Catholic Messenger* (Davenport), "is that none of us has any future, but each of us must live through eternity. It is a fact that our spirits will live forever. Since tomorrow does not exist for anyone, Almighty God must constantly provide for renewal of the conditions which permit us to live on earth .... If suddenly the world ends, as indeed it could, will there be a population explosion in heaven, or will there be standing room only in hell?"

Life is eternal; and love is immortal; And death is only a horizon; and a horizon is nothing more save the limit of our sight.
—Rossiter Worthington Raymond

I have never seen what to me seemed an atom of proof that there is a future life. And yet—I am strongly inclined to expect one.
—Mark Twain

Without the hope of an after-life, this life is not even worth the effort of getting dressed in the morning.
—Bismarck

If you were to destroy in mankind the belief in immortality, not only love but every living force maintaining the life of the world would at once be dried up.
—Brothers Karamazov

The only secret people keep is Immortality.
—Emily Dickinson

Philosophy of Life

There's night and day, brother, both sweet things; sun, moon, and stars, brother, all sweet things; there's a wind on the heath. Life is very sweet, brother, who would wish to die?
—George Bernanos

I shall tell you a great secret, my friend. Do not wait for the last judgment. It takes place every day.
   —Albert Camus

Man's unhappiness, as I construe, comes of his greatness; it is because there is an infinite in him, which with all his cunning he cannot quite bury under the finite.
   —Thomas Carlyle

These be
Three silent things:
The falling snow ... the hour
Before the dawn ... the mouth of one
Just dead.
   —Adelaide Crapsey, adapted from *Cinquain: Triad*

A thing of beauty is a joy forever:
Its loveliness increases; it will never
Pass into nothingness; but still will keep
A bower quiet for us, and a sleep
Full of sweet dreams, and health, and quiet breathing.
   —John Keats, adapted from *Endymion*

And were an epitaph to be my story
I'd have a short one ready for my own.
I would have written of me on my stone:
I had a lover's quarrel with the world.
   —Robert Frost

Don't hurry, don't worry. You're here for a short visit. So be sure to stop and smell the flowers.
   —Walter C. Hagen

There is always inequity in life. Some men are killed in war and some men are wounded, and some men never leave the country ... Life is unfair.
—John F. Kennedy, press conference, 21 March 1962

All interest in diseases and death is only another expression of interest in life.
—Thomas Mann, from *The Magic Mountain*

Time cools, time clarifies; no mood can be maintained quite unaltered through the course of hours.
—Thomas Mann

The one who goes is happier, than those he leaves behind.
—Edward Pollock

The highest reward for man's toil is not what he gets for it, but what he becomes by it.
—John Ruskin

You have suffered worse things; god will put amend to these also.
—Virgil

Love moves the sun in the heavens and all the stars.
—Dante, from *Divine Comedy*

The greater pleasure in life is to do a good deed in secret and have it discovered by accident.
—Charles Lamb, from *Table Talk in the Athenaeum*

When religion submits to reason it begins to die.
—Will Durant

Age is a thing of mind over matter—if you don't mind, it don't matter.
—Mark Twain

That best portion of a good man's life, His little nameless unremembered acts of kindness and love.

—William Wordsworth, from *Lines Composed a Few Miles above Tintern Abbey*

Everyone in the world is Christ and they are crucified.

—Sherwood Anderson

A lifetime of happiness! No man alive could bear it; it would be hell on earth.

—George Bernard Shaw

There are two tragedies in life. One is to lose your heart's desire. The other is to gain it.

—George Bernard Shaw

As I grow to understand life less and less, I learn to love it more and more.

—Jules Renard

O God! It is a fearful thing,
To see a human soul take wing
In any shape, in any mood.
What is the worst of woes that wait on age?
What stamps the wrinkle deeper in the brow?
To view each loved one blotted from life's page,
And be alone on earth, as I am now.

—Lord Byron

And no one exists alone;
Hunger allows no choice
To the citizen or the police;
We must love one another or die.

—W. H. Auden

We are all in the same boat and we are all seasick.
—G. K. Chesterton

We began this sermon with a reference to Winston Churchill. I should like to close with an incident about this same man. It took place ten years before his death in 1965. Billy Graham was in the midst of his Greater London Crusade, and although the Prime Minister had not chosen to attend the Crusade itself, he did consent to allowing Mr. Graham a five-minute interview with him. So, at the stroke of noon on the appointed day, the Evangelist was shown into the Cabinet Room. Sir Winston stood at the center of the long Cabinet table, an unlighted cigar in his hand. Billy was surprised to see how short a man he was. Sir Winston motioned Billy to be seated, and said he had been reading about him, and was most happy to have him come, because, as the Prime Minister put it, "we need this emphasis." Then, he asked Mr. Graham a most important question. Thereupon, quite predictable, Billy pulled out his little New Testament, and answered: "Mr. Prime Minister, I am filled with hope."
—Adapted from *The Black Dog and the Morning Star* (Treasure Island, Fla.: Cathedral Publishers, 1975) by Henry S. Date

What will they put on your tombstone? What is it that you hold so near and dear to your heart that everyone who knows you knows you treasure it? Whatever it is, get out there for the world to see and enjoy! It is said that we make a living by what we get, but we make a life by what we give. What are you giving? I want to teach my niece to always keep a song in her heart, to use music as a vehicle of emotion. I want her to know that it's okay to look at the important people in her life—her parents, her grandparents, her Aunt Sandy—and say, "Have I told you lately that I love you?" and turn to her little brother and her buddies to say—"Thank you for being my friends!"
—Sandra Call Wilder, adapted from an address entitled "I Believe in Music" (15 May 1996)

Preaching

It is one of the proofs of the divinity of the gospel that the preaching of it has survived.
—Woodrow Wilson

I remember my first funeral, at St. Joseph's in Quincy. I came back to the rectory with tears in my eyes, and the pastor—Monsignor Allston, a great man—took me aside and said, "Father, if you want to survive, stop that right now! Toward the dead, you must be dead to yourself."
—Parish Priest (*The New Yorker* [13 June 1988]: 39)

Public speaking sometimes is more feared than death. The Book of Lists reports public speaking as the number-one fear among those surveyed, while death came in fourth. Comedian Jerry Seinfeld has concluded from this that at a funeral, most people would rather be lying in the coffin than giving the eulogy.
—*Washingtonian Magazine* (March 1996)

An effective preacher brings out great love or great hostility, toward Jesus first and toward the preacher secondarily. But no one goes to sleep.
—Rev. John B. Healey (*America* [26 November 1988]: 438)

The world is waiting for those who love it; if you don't love the world, don't preach to it: preach to yourself.
—Vincent McNabb

Preaching is heady wine. It is pleasant to tell people exactly where they get off.
—Arnold Lunn, from *Now I See*

Christ said not to His first assembly: Go and preach trifles to the world; but give to them the true foundation.
—Dante, from *Paradiso*, canto 29

Kind words are the music of the world. They have a power that seems to be beyond the natural causes as though they were some angel's song which had lost its way and come back to earth.

When I heard that Dorothy Day, founder of the Catholic Worker Movement, had died at the age of 83, I thought with pity of the poor priest faced with the impossible task of doing justice to such a truly great woman in the brief space of her funeral eulogy.
—Msgr. George G. Higgins

It is always dangerous to go to church, for there is always a chance that God's word will break through the protective shell Americans have built up.
—William Sloan Coffin

On the morning before the funeral the President said that he had no plans to give a eulogy the next day. "God, no. I couldn't do it. I would choke up. I would be permanently ensconced as a member of the Bawl Patrol. I can't. I'm terrible at those things. I've had trouble paying my respects to the fallen soldiers on the *Iowa*, or the dead out of Desert Storm, without getting emotional. I'd love to, but I know my limitations. I even got choked up here at Camp David last night. We had our choir singing. We had a little vespers program with Amy Grant. It was so beautiful, and I found myself choking up. We had a bunch of friends up here, and 'Oh God,' I said, 'please hold back the floods.'"
—from an interview with President George Bush on the death of his mother (*The New Yorker* [7 December 1992])

Why should good words ne'er be said of a friend till he is dead?
—Daniel Webster Hoyt, from *A Sermon in Rhyme*

In *Life* magazine author Morris L. West began a piece on the death of the beloved Pope John XXIII by asking, "Will they canonize him and make him officially a saint in the calendar? In a way I hope not .... Good Lord why not? I want to remember him for what he was—a loving man, a simple priest, a good pastor and a builder of bridges

across which we poor devils may hope to scramble one day for salvation."
—Jay Cormier

On another occasion preacher Prescott averts crisis with sage humor. Facing the task of laying to rest a lost sheep who, by the parson's own count, had smashed every one of the Ten Commandments, Preacher Prescott stands up to deliver a funeral oration over the blackened soul, suddenly bangs shut his Bible and declaims: "Brothers and Sisters, you know Charlie. I know Charlie. Let's bury him. Amen." And so they did.

Clergymen preach about many subjects, but the congregation generally prefers them to preach about half an hour.

The more a preacher appeases, the more he pleases.

The preacher who fills his church every Sunday is the one who tells you how to live rather than how to die.

Few sinners are saved after the first twenty minutes of a sermon.
—Mark Twain

Americans are so tense and keyed up that it is impossible even to put them to sleep with a sermon.
—Norman Vincent Peale

The eternal gospel does not require an everlasting sermon.

When Frederick William Faber preached the panegyric of St. Ignatius Loyola on the occasion of the feast of the founder of the Jesuits, he spent an hour in unbroken, sympathetic, indeed fervent expositions of this Saint's spirituality, and only in the last sentence did he introduce the necessary limitation and expansion: "This, then,

my dear Brethren, is St. Ignatius's way to heaven, and thank God, it is not the only way."
—Baron Von Hugel, adapted from *The Life of Prayer*

Purpose of Life

When Victor Frankl of Vienna, a survivor of the holocaust, spoke in Louisville he told of a grieving general practitioner whose wife had died two years before. For those two years he remained in a deep depression because of his intense love for his wife. He asked Frankl for help. Frankl confronted him with this question: "What would have happened, Doctor, if you had died first, and your wife would have had to survive you?" "Oh," he replied, "for her this would have been terrible; how she would have suffered!" Then Frankl said, "You see, Doctor, such a suffering has been spared her, and it was you who have spared her this suffering; but now, you have to pay for it by surviving and mourning her." The Doctor said nothing. But shook Frankl's hand and left. The man's life has meaning that he had not seen before, and the prospect of recovery was real.
—Victor Frankl, adapted from "Man's Search for Meaning,"
   Existential Psychotherapy

When a man does not know what harbor he is making for, no wind is the right wind.
—Seneca

Our critical day is not the very day of our death, but the whole course of our life. I thank him that prays for me when the bell tolls, but I thank him much more that catechizes me, or preaches to me, or instructs me how to live.
—John Donne, from *Death's Duel*

We are standing beside the coffin of a man beloved. For the last time, his life, his battles, his sufferings, and his purpose pass before the mind's eye. At this solemn and stirring moment, our tears are gripped by a voice which we seldom or never hear above the deafening traffic

of mundane affairs. "What's next?" It says. What is life, and what is death? Have we any continuing existence? Is it all an empty dream, or has this life of ours, and our death, a meaning? If we are
to go on living, we must answer this question ...
   —Gustav Mahler's comment on his great composition about
      death and resurrection, *The Second Symphony*

We trust that somehow good
Will be the final goal of all
That nothing walks with aimless feet;
That not one life shall be destroy'd
Or cast as rubbish to the void,
When God hath made the file complete.
   —Lord Tennyson

Facing death means facing the ultimate question of the meaning of life. If we really want to live, we must have the courage to recognize that ultimately life is very short and that everything we do counts.
   —Elizabeth Kubler-Ross, adapted from *A Manual of Death
      Education*

Out of every tragedy can come a blessing or a curse, compassion or bitterness—the choice is yours.
   —Elizabeth Kubler-Ross

If you would indeed behold the spirit of death, open your heart unto the body of life. For life and death are one, even as the river and the sea are one.
   —Kahlil Gibran, from *The Prophet*

This life is much too much trouble, far too strange, to arrive at the end of it and then to be asked what you make of it, and have to answer, "Scientific Humanism." That won't do. A poor show. Life is a mystery. Love is a delight. Therefore I take it as axiomatic that one should settle for nothing less than the infinite mystery and the delight, i.e., GOD. In fact, I demand it.
—Walker Percy, from an interview in *Esquire*

Resurrection

The root of all good works is the hope of the resurrection; for the expectation of the reward nerves the soul to good works.
—St. Cyril of Jerusalem, from *Catechetical Discourse*

The bodies of the saints will therefore rise again from every defect, from every deformity, as well as from every corruption, encumbrance, or hindrance. In this respect their freedom of action will be as complete as their happiness; and for this reason their bodies have been called 'spiritual,' though undoubtedly they will be bodies and not spirits.
—St. Augustine, from *Enchiridion*

All you that weep, all you that mourn,
All you that grieving go,
Lift up your eyes, your heads adorn,
Put off your weeds of woe.
The sorrows of the Passion week
Like tearful dreams are fled.
For He hath triumphed Whom you seek,
Is risen—that was dead.
—Henry Longan Stuart, from *Resurrexit*

In her letters in the Habit of Being, Flannery O'Connor writes about the resurrection, "For my part I think that when I know the laws of the flesh are, then I will know what God is. For me it is the virgin birth, the incarnation and the resurrection which are the true laws of

121

the flesh. I am always astonished at the emphasis the Church puts on the body. It is not the soul that shall rise but it is this body, your body—crucified, of course, because Christ is glorified in His body. We are to look forward to a resurrection of the body which will be flesh and spirit united in peace."

Pagans believe in the death of Jesus; Christians believe in his resurrection.
   —St. Augustine

Saving the body is not a trick for resurrectionists. The Bible says that this finite body, this limited history, is inherently an ingredient of the divine. Living this life in the overweight body is already living eternal life. Christian resurrection offers not a continuation of what a Platonist already regards as a second-rate; resurrection is the assertion that the supposed limitation of a human life is already overcome. Resurrection in Christianity does not mean continuation of the limited; it means fulfillment of the limited. My three score ten is all my life that I have—there is no "to be continued" marker on the gravestone. In Christianity every death is a definitive death, and one can legitimately mourn at the shortness of it all. What Christianity says in the notion of resurrection is that this finite and definitive life is not continued but amplified. It is as if life were one tune and when it is done that is the tune—there is no second movement. But God orchestrates life's jingle into eternity; hence the importance of this life for "heaven" or "hell."
   —George Dennis O'Brien, from *God and the New Haven Railroad*
      (Boston: Beacon Press)

Every parting gives a foretaste of death; every coming together again a foretaste of the resurrection.
   —Arthur Schopenhauer

The smallest sprout shows there is really no death.
   —Walt Whitman

Let us consider, beloved, how the Lord is continually revealing to us the resurrection that is to be. Of this He has constituted the Lord Jesus Christ the first fruits, by raising Him from the dead.
—Pope St. Clement I

If a man born among infidels and barbarians does what lies in his power God will reveal to him what is necessary for salvation, either by inward inspiration or by sending him a preacher of the faith.
—St. Thomas Aquinas, from *Summa theologica*

God wills all men to be saved that are saved, not because there is no man whom He does not wish saved, but because there is no man saved whose salvation He does not will.
—St. Augustine, from *De praedestinatione sanctorum*

The bodies of the saints will therefore rise again free from every defect, from every deformity, as well as free from every corruption, encumbrance, or hindrance. In this respect their freedom of action will be as complete as their happiness; and for this reason their bodies have been called "spiritual," though undoubtedly they will be bodies and not spirits.
—St. Augustine, adapted from *Enchiridion*

The Church calls this "something" the "Resurrection of Jesus from the death." Dietrich Bonfoeffer has warned the church not to ask too many "how?" and "what?" questions. Such advice is well taken whenever we consider an Eastertide, for the New Testament itself never attempts to explain exactly what happened. As far as we know, there were no eyewitnesses to the actual event. Albert Schweitzer is profoundly correct when he says, "Christianity is not a formula for explaining everything." Scientific analysis is correctly interested in explaining but the Christian faith is interested in transformation!
—adapted from *Recognizing the Resurrected* (Cathedral Publishers) by Roland P. Perdue

Soul

The soul we define to be sprung from the breath of God, immortal, possessing body, having form, simple in its substance, intelligent in its own nature, developing its power in various ways, free in its determinations, subject to the changes of accident, in its faculties mutable, rational, supreme, endued with an instinct of presentiment, evolved out of one.

—Tertullian, adapted from *Treatise on the Soul*

If, again we were to define man as to say, Man is a rational substance consisting of mind and body, then without doubt man has a soul that is not body, and a body that is not a soul.

—St. Augustine, from *De trinitate*

For the soul is the inner face of man, by which we are known, that we may be regarded with love by our Maker.

—Pope Gregory I, from *Morals*

Every holy soul is itself heaven in a sense—a heaven with understanding for its sun, faith for its moon, and virtues for its stars, a heaven where God dwells, according to His faithful promise. We will come unto him and make our abode with him.

—St. Bernard, adapted from *Sermons on the Canticle of Canticles*

The mind is a subsisting form, and is consequently immortal. Aristotle agrees that the mind is divine and perpetual.

—St. Thomas Aquinas, quoted in *De anima* 1,6

In the most noble part of the soul, the domain of our spiritual powers, we are constituted in the form of a living and eternal mirror of God; we bear in it the imprint of His eternal image and no other image can enter there.

—Jan van Ruysbroeck, from *Mirror of Eternal Salvation*

He must have little spirit who thinks that a spirit is nothing.
  —St. Bernard

The soul of man is larger than the sky,
Deeper than ocean, or the abysmal dark
Of the unfathomed center.
  —David Hartley Coleridge

Either dead is a state of nothingness and utter unconsciousness, or, as men say, there is a change and migration of the soul from this world to another .... Now if death be of such a nature, I say
that to die is to gain, for eternity is then only a single night.
  —Plato

He who created you without your will, will not justify you without your will.
  —St. Augustine

Thus, the "personality" or the "psyche" or the "mind," call it what you will, of a person, is something quite other, and different, from the mere arrangement and chromosomes of the body—something beyond these, a unifying and identifying element we should not hesitate to call "spirit."
  —Sidney J. Harris, from "For the Time Being," *Detroit Free Press*
  (1 October 1974)

Appendix B

Poetic Sequiturs

Builders of Eternity

Isn't it strange that princes and kings
and clowns that caper in sawdust rings,
and ordinary folks like you and me
are builders of eternity.

To each is given a bag of tools,
an hour-glass and a book of rules;
and each must build, ere time is flown,
a stumbling block or a stepping stone.
   —Anonymous

I Did Not Die

Forgive me and forgive those
that trespass against me.
Do not stand at my grave and weep.
I am not there, I do not sleep.

I am the thousand winds that blow.
I am the diamond glints on snow.
I am the sunlight on ripened grain.
I am the gentle autumnal rain.

When you waken in the morning hush
I am the soft uplifting rush
of quiet birds in circled flight.
I am the soft stars that shine at night.

Do not stand at my grave and cry.
I am not there.
I did not die.
    —Anonymous

The Devil Is a Gentleman

The devil is a gentleman, and asks you down to stay
At his little place at what's its name (it isn't far away).
They say the sport is splendid; there is always something new,
And lovely scenes, and fearful feats that none but he can do;
He can shoot the feathered cherubs if they fly on his estate,
Or fish for Father Neptune with mermaids for a bait;
He scaled amid the staggering stars that precipice the sky,
And blew his trumpet above heaven, and got by mastery
And starry crown of God Himself, and shoved it on the shelf;
But the devil is a gentleman, and doesn't brag himself.
O blind your eyes and break your heart and hack your hand away,
And lose your love and shave your head; but do not go to stay
At the little place in what's its name where folks are rich and clever;
The golden and the goodly house, where things grow worse forever;
There are things you need not known of, though you live
    and die in vain,
There are souls more sick of pleasure that you are sick of pain;
There is a game of April fool that's played behind the door,
Where the fool remains forever and the April comes no more,
Where the splendor of the daylight grows drearier than the dark,
And life droops like a vulture that once was such a lark;
And that is the Blue Devil that once was the Blue Bird;
For the devil is a gentleman, and doesn't keep his word.
    —G. K. Chesterton (*Notre Dame University Religious Bulletin*,
        vol. XL, no.14 [24 October 1960]).

Death of a Child

"I'll lend you for a little while,
a child of mine," God said,
"for you to cherish while he lives,
and mourn for when he's dead.
It may be six or seven years,
Or only two or three,
but will you, till I call him home,
look after him for me?
He'll bring his love to gladden you
and should his stay be brief,
you'll have a host of memories
as solace for your grief.
I cannot promise he will stay
since all from earth return,
but there are lessons taught below
I want this child to learn.
I've looked the wide world over
in my search for teachers true
and, from the throng
that crowd life's lane
at last I've chosen you.
Now will you give him all your love,
nor think your labor vain,
and turn against me when I come
to take him back again?"
   —from *Comfort for the Bereaved* 13

Letting Go

To "let go" does not mean to stop caring; it means you can't do it
  for someone else,
To "let go" is not to cut yourself off; it is the realization you
can't control another.
To "let go" is not to enable, but to allow learning from natural
  consequences.
To "let go" is to admit powerlessness, which means the outcome
  is not in your hands.
To "let go" is not to try to change or blame another; it's to make the
  most of yourself.
To "let go" is not to care for, but to care about.
To "let go" is not to fix, but to be supportive.
To "let go" is not to judge, but to allow another to be a human being.
To "let go" is not to be in the middle, arranging all of the outcomes,
but to allow others to affect their own destinies.
To "let go" is not to deny, but to accept.
To "let go" is not to nag, scold or argue,
but instead to search out your shortcomings and correct them.
To "let go" is not to adjust everything to your desires,
but to take each day as it comes and cherish yourself in it.
To "let go" is not to regret the past, but to grow and live for the future.
To "let go" is to fear less and love more.
  —Author Unknown, from *Catholic Universe Bulletin*, 1997

Come In

As I came to the edge of the woods,
Thrush music—hark!
Now if it was dusk outside,
Inside it was dark.

Too dark in the woods for a bird
By sleight of wing
To better its perch for the night,
Though it still could sing.

The last of the light of the sun
That had died in the west
Still lived for one song more
In a thrush's breast.

Far in the pillared dark
Thrush music went—
Almost like a call to come in
To the dark and lament.

But no, I was out for stars:
I would not come in.
I meant not even if asked,
And I hadn't been.
   —Robert Frost

The genius of Robert Frost is modeled in this poem. There are two interpretations: the obvious one of a thrush in the woods and the deeper meaning of death. "As I come to the edge of the woods" means "to die." "By sleight of wing" symbolizes the last rites of the Church. "Too dark in the woods" refers to the afterlife.

Lament

Listen, children;
Your father is dead.
From his old coats
I'll make you little jackets;
I'll make you little trousers
From his old pants.
There'll be in his pockets
Things he used to put there,
Keys and pennies
Covered with tobacco;
Dan shall have the pennies
To save in his bank;
Anne shall have the keys
To make a pretty noise with.
Life must go on,
Though good men die;
Anne, eat your breakfast;
Life must go on;
I forget just why.
        —Edna St. Vincent Millay

The Dream of Gerontius

It is the face of the Incarnate God
Shall smite thee with that keen and subtle pain;
And yet the memory which it leaves will be
A sovereign febrifuge to heal the wound;
And yet withal it will the wound provoke,
And aggravate and widen it the more.
When, then, (if such thy lot), thou seest thy Judge,
The sight of Him will kindle in thy heart
All tender, gracious, reverential thoughts.
Thou wilt be sick with love, and yearn for Him,
And feel as though thou couldst but pity Him,
That one so sweet should e'er have placed Himself
At disadvantage such, as to be used
So vilely by a being so vile as thee.
There is a pleading in His pensive eyes,
Will pierce thee to the quick, and trouble thee.
And thou wilt hate and loathe thyself; for, though
Now sinless, thou wilt feel that thou hast sinned,
As never didst thou feel; and wilt desire
To slink away, and hide thee from His sight;
And yet wilt have a longing aye to dwell
Within the beauty of His countenance.
And these two pains, so counter and so keen,—
The longing for Him, when thou seest Him not;
The shame of self at thought of seeing Him,—
Will be thy veriest, sharpest purgatory.
   —Cardinal Newman

Hamlet, Act I, Scene V

The ghost speaks to Hamlet:

"I am thy father's spirit;
Doom'd for a certain term to walk the night,
And for the day confined to fast in fires,
Till the four crimes done in my days of nature
Are burnt and purged away. But that I am forbid
To tell the secrets of my prison-house,
I could a tale unfold whose lightest word
Would harrow up thy soul, freeze thy young blood,
Make thy two eyes, like stars, start from their spheres,
Thy knotted and combined locks to part,
And each particular hair to stand on end,
Like quills upon the fretful porcupine:
But this eternal blazon must not be
To ears of flesh and blood. List, List, O List!
Of thou didst ever thy dear father love."
    —Shakespeare

Shakespeare knew the teaching of the church on purgatory. His "Timon of Athens" suggests at least some distant familiarity with Greek beliefs (as in the Greek play *Antigone*). The ghost of Hamlet's father offers a fittingly uninviting view of purgatory, whether or not with Greek tragic coloration.

Resurrection

Me? Rise again?
This lamentable person
This disappointer
This promise breaker
This high-weeping self avenger
This schemer of short cuts
To undeserved gains
This fraudulent lover
This side-stepper of injustice
This fun-seeker amid the
Cries of the hungry and lonely
This back door escape artist
From your "follow Me"
This spend thrift you loved
And called and went alone
To the cross for
Who? Me? Rise Again?

If so, not that old lamentable
Person, Lord—
But a new one—like Yourself
Like the new self I never quite became
Here, with all my efforts and Yours
Bury the old me, Jesus
Raise the new one, O Christ
You can do it
You can kill this death
That is killing me
You can bring me to life again
You can bring me to life again
You can bring me to life
You can. Alleluia! Amen
  —Anonymous

Children of God

Unless the grain of wheat ... (Jn 12:24)
There once was a seed
Who didn't want to grow.
He wanted to stay
In the dark down below.
He stretched himself upwards
With all his might
And burst through the earth
To the air and the light.
And he danced with the others
For many an hour
No longer a seed
But a beautiful flower.
    —Christy Kenneally (*Furrow* [February 1988])

Immortality

I came from nothing; but from where
Come the undying thoughts I bear?
Down, through long links of death and birth,
From the past poets of the earth,
My immortality is there.
Before this life began to be,
The happy songs that wake in me
Woke long ago and far apart.
Heavily on this little heart
Presses this immortality.
    —Meynell, from "A Song of Derivations,"

Crossing of the Bar

Sunset and evening star,
And one clear call for me!
And may there be no moaning at the bar,
When I put out to sea,
But such a tide as moving seems asleep,
Too full for sound and foam,
When that which drew from out the boundless deep
Turns again home.

Twilight and evening bell,
And after that the dark!
And say there be no sadness of farewell,
When I embark;
For tho' from out our bourne of time and place
The flood may bear me far,
I hope to see my Pilot face to face.
When I have crost the bar.

   —Tennyson

Returning to God

We are born in exile and die there too.
as soon as we set sail on the great voyage of life,
we begin our return.
we spend our lives dreaming
of a homeland we have never seen.
like homing birds that are released in a strange country,
and know no rest until they return home,
so it is with us.
When we die,
we do not so much go to God
as return to him.

   —*Funeral Liturgies*

The Clock of Life

The clock of life is wound but once,
And no one has the power
To tell just when the hands will stop
At late or early hour.
Now is the only time you own.
Live, live, toil with a will,
Place no faith in tomorrow
For the clock may then be still.
 —F. B. Meyer

Hamlet, Act III, Scene I

To be or not to be: that is the question:
Whether 'tis nobler in the mind to suffer
The slings and arrows of outrageous fortune,
Or to take arms against a sea of troubles,
And by opposing end them? To die: to sleep;
No more; and, by a sleep to say we end
The heart-ache and the thousand natural shocks
That flesh is heir to, 'tis a consummation
Devoutly to be wish'd. To die, to sleep;
To sleep; perchance to dream: ay, there's the rub;
For in that sleep of death what dreams may come
When we have shuffled off this mortal coil
Must give us pause.
 —Shakespeare

Hamlet, Act I, Scene II

O! that this too too solid flesh would melt,
Thaw and resolve itself into the dew;
Or that the Everlasting had not fix'd
His canon 'gainst self-slaughter! O God! O God!
How weary, stale, flat, and unprofitable
Seem to me all the uses of this world.
—Shakespeare

Selected Works Cited and Recommended

Homilies and Homily Illustrations

Bartlett, David L. *Between the Bible and the Church: New Methods for Biblical Preaching.* Nashville: Abingdon Press, 1999.

Bausch, William J. *Timely Homilies: The Wit and Wisdom of an Ordinary Pastor.* Mystic, Conn. Twenty-Third Publications, 1990.

Bausch, William J. *A World of Stories for Preachers and Teachers.* Mystic, Conn.: Twenty-Third Publications, 1998.

Bernstein, Eleanor, CSJ, ed. *Liturgical Words, Gestures, Objects.* Notre Dame: Notre Dame Center for Pastoral Liturgy: 1995.

Deffner, Donald L. *Windows into the Lectionary: Seasonal Anecdotes for Preaching and Teaching.* San Jose: Resource Publications, Inc., 1996.

Foley, Edward. *Preaching Basics.* Chicago: Liturgy Training Publications, 1998.

Henderschedt, James L. *The Dream Catcher: 20 Lectionary-Based Stories for Teaching and Preaching.* San Jose: Resource Publications, Inc., 1996.

Karaban, Roslyn A., and Deni Mack. *Extraordinary Preaching: 20 Homilies by Roman Catholic Women.* San Jose: Resource Publications, Inc., 1996.

Master Sermon Series. 5 vols. Royal Oak, Mich.: Cathedral Publishers, 1970–1974.

National Conference of Catholic Bishops. *Fulfilled in Your Hearing: The Homily in the Sunday Assembly.* Washington, D.C.: United States Catholic Conference, 1982.

Papineau, Andre. *Sermons for Sermon Haters.* San Jose: Resource Publications, Inc., 1992.

Parachini, Patricia A. *Lay Preaching: State of the Question.* Collegeville: The Liturgical Press, 1999.

Philippart, David. *Saving Signs, Wondrous Words.* Chicago: Liturgy Training Publications, 1996.

Pilch, John J. *The Cultural World of Jesus: Sunday by Sunday (Cycles A, B & C).* Collegeville: The Liturgical Press, 1995.

Troeger, Thomas H. *Borrowed Light*. Oxford: University Press, 1994.

———. *Ten Strategies for Preaching in a Multi Media Culture*. Nashville: Abingdon Press, 1996.

Untener, Ken. *Preaching Better: Practical Suggestions for Homilists*. New York: Paulist Press, 1999.

Waznak, Robert. *An Introduction to the Homily*. Collegeville: Liturgical Press, 1998.

Funeral Liturgies

Aridas, Chris. *The Catholic Funeral: The Church's Ministry of Hope*. New York: Crossroad Pub Co., 1998.

Boyer, Mark G. *Baptized into Christ's Death and Resurrection: Preparing to Celebrate a Christian Funeral*. Collegeville, Minn.: Liturgical Press, 1999.

Engle, Paul E. *Baker's Funeral Handbook: Resources for Pastors*. Grand Rapids: Baker Book House, 1996.

Fader, Barbara M. *Blessed Are Those Who Mourn: Personalized Prayers of the Faithful for the Funeral Rite*. Notre Dame: Ave Maria Press, 1998.

McCarthy, Flor. *Funeral Liturgies*. Dublin, Ireland: Dominican Publications, 1994.

Order of Christian Funerals. Washington, D.C.: International Committee on English in the Liturgy, 1989.

Smith, Margaret Bayard. *Facing Death Together: Parish Funerals*. Chicago: Liturgy Training Publications, 1999.

Death & Grieving

Anderson, H., and E. Foley. *Mighty Stories, Dangerous Rituals: Weaving Together the Human and the Divine*. San Francisco: Jossey-Bass, 1998.

Brueggemann, W. *The Message of the Psalms*. Minneapolis: Augsburg Publishing House, 1984.

Christensen, M. J. *The Samaritan's Imperative: Compassionate Ministry to People Living with AIDS*. Nashville: Abingdon Press, 1991.

Clemons, T. *What Does the Bible Say about Suicide?* Minneapolis: Fortress Press, 1990.

Comfort for the Bereaved. London: Catholic Truth Society, 1980.

Crenshaw, D. A. *Bereavement: Counseling the Grieving Throughout the Life Cycle*. New York: Continuum, 1990.

Feifel, H. "Psychology and Death: Meaningful Recovery." In *The Path Ahead: Readings in Death and Dying*, edited by L. A. DeSpelder and A. L. Strickland, 19–28. Mountain View, Calif.: Mayfield Pub. Co., 1995.

Herman, J. L. *Trauma and Recovery*. New York: Basic Books, 1992.

Hoff, L. A. *People in Crisis: Understanding and Helping*. 4th ed. San Francisco: Jossey-Bass, 1995.

Karaban, Roslyn A. *Complicated Losses, Difficult Deaths: A Practical Guide for Ministering to Grievers*. San Jose: Resource Publications, Inc., 2000.

Morgan, Ernest. *A Manual of Death Education & Simple Burial*. Burnsville, N.C.: 1980.

Papenbrock, P., and R. F. Voss. *How to Help the Child Whose Parent Has Died*. Redmond, Wash.: Medic Pub. Co., 1988.

Sloyan, Virginia, ed. *A Sourcebook about Christian Death*. Chicago: Liturgy Training Publications, 1990.

Speece, M. W., and S. B. Brent. "The Development of Children's Understanding of Death." In *Handbook of Childhood Death and Bereavement*, edited by C. A. Corr and D. M. Corr, 29–50. New York: Springer, 1996.

Staudacher, C. *Men and Grief*. Oakland, Calif.: New Harbinger Pub., 1991.

Sunderland, R. *Getting Through Grief: Caregiving by Congregations*. Nashville: Abingdon, 1993.

Williams, Donna Reilly, and JoAnn Sturzl. *Grief Ministry: Helping Others Mourn*. Rev. ed. San Jose: Resource Publications, Inc., 1992.